TURNING
FORTY
IN THE
EIGHTIES

ALSO BY MICHAEL P. NICHOLS

Family Therapy: Concepts and Methods

Catharsis and Psychotherapy, with M. Zax

Emotional Expression in Psychotherapy, with R. Pierce
and J. DuBrin

*The Basic Techniques of Psychodynamic Psychotherapy:
Foundations of Clinical Practice,* with T. Paolino

TURNING FORTY IN THE EIGHTIES

Personal Crisis,
Time for Change

Michael P. Nichols

W. W. Norton & Company · New York · London

Copyright © 1986 by Michael P. Nichols
All rights reserved.
Published simultaneously in Canada by Penguin Books Canada Ltd,
2801 John Street, Markham, Ontario L3R 1B4
Printed in the United States of America.

The text of this book is composed in Avanta, with display type set in Litho Light.
Composition and manufacturing by The Haddon Craftsmen, Inc.
Book design by Bernard Klein.

Library of Congress Cataloging-in-Publication Data
Nichols, Michael P.
    Turning forty in the eighties.
    Bibliography: p. 273
    Includes index.
    1. Middle age. 2. Maturation (Psychology)
    3. Life change events. 1. Title.
HQ1059.4.N52 1986 305.2′44 85-21396

ISBN 0-393-02266-8

W. W. Norton & Company, Inc., 500 Fifth Avenue, New York, N. Y. 10110
W. W. Norton & Company Ltd., 37 Great Russell Street, London WC1B 3NU
    2 3 4 5 6 7 8 9 0

To Bob Pierce and Jay Efran,
uncommon teachers and treasured friends.

Contents

Author's Note

THIS is a book about the sometimes painful transition to maturity. The unsettling realization that the future is now and it isn't what we expected ushers in an interlude of uneasiness. A personal crisis occurs when we can no longer suppress nebulous fears and unsatisfied longings. It usually occurs somewhere between the ages of thirty-five and forty-five, but for some reason thirty-seven seems to be a magic number, close enough to forty to have to face middle age, but too soon to have come to terms with it. My aim is to describe how the difficulty arises, why it persists, and how it may be resolved. I will attempt to explain why so many people scoff at the idea of a "midlife crisis"; why they deny so forcefully that they might have a crisis; and how, so often, the midlife crisis is masked or delayed.

The book is addressed to men *and* women. Some writers have considered the midlife crisis a man's problem, the result of frustration in a career that was given too much importance. Since most men's lives do revolve around their work, their crises commonly take a similar form: somewhere around the age of thirty-seven, a man begins to question the emphasis on work to provide meaning and satisfaction. Because women's lives are complicated by a greater variety of roles, their crises come at varying times and are as likely to involve personal relationships as career frustrations. This diversity makes mid-life crisis for women harder to describe and harder to antici-pate.

While it is possible to create a more passionate life, with deeper commitments and more intimate relationships, by age forty most people are well practiced at running away—from themselves and from other people. Some people lapse into complacency and cynicism. Others rationalize their difficulties and build out of them a defensive compromise with life. Fear, not lack of imagination, explains why so many settle for "com-panionate marriages" and unfulfilling jobs. Deep hurts wound the spirit and condition avoidance. Changing the habits of a lifetime is hard. Unless we understand what needs to be changed and what constitutes a rewarding life, our efforts to resolve crisis are likely to be directed toward the path of least resistance.

Unhappy people tend to locate their distress in the external circumstances that provoke it—trouble at work, stress in the family, decline in energy—rather than recognize the personal vulnerability that lies much deeper. Even the experts advise people who want to find themselves to look outside themselves.

Many frustrated forty-year-olds gladly adopt some new pas-sion to take their minds off of their situations. Some of these "magnificent obsessions" are manifestly destructive—the fling that breaks up the family, the weekend drinking binges that begin to encroach on the workweek. Other responses seem constructive, but because they don't address the basic problem they forestall real change. Various escapist outlets let people blow off steam, but do nothing to break down the tight walls of self-imposed restriction.

Nowadays people writing about midlife draw attention to the need to readjust life structures—patterns of work and family life—worked out in the twenties and thirties. This writing serves a useful function; people at midlife *do* need to reevaluate their careers and family lives to insure security and satisfaction in the second half of life. Unfortunately, these assessments are often made with little or no self-knowledge. Disappointed men and women may think of changing mates or changing careers. Few think of changing themselves.

Midlife is a time of taking stock, yet the reassessment is incomplete unless it includes insight into the essential personality and family dynamics of the individual. People invest themselves in their work or children to give meaning and purpose to their lives. These commitments are extensions of the self and cannot easily be renounced. It is all very well to criticize the compulsion to succeed or the practice of self-denying submission, but we are driven by unconscious motives— for love and self-affirmation—from which many of us cannot emancipate ourselves. As long as a significant amount of mental energy is tied up in conflict, it is not available for investment in new projects. Similarly, we cannot become more intimate with families or friends as long as we are held in check by a primal fear of closeness. Pretending to surrender to love is not the same as doing so; it is only a timid truce.

My own background in psychoanalysis and family therapy helped me to understand some of the factors complicating the transition to middle age. We cannot assess our lives without knowing what is inside; and we cannot know what is inside if we imagine ourselves in isolation. I will describe the effects of adult midlife crises on the rest of the family, using examples from the lives of real men and women. This section will help readers recognize the importance of discovering the self—the basic personality—and will provide practical strategies for enriching relationships with others. My main purpose is to clarify the experience of personal crisis, but in the process I also hope to contribute to a much-needed integration of individual psychology and family systems theory.

Some people can make constructive changes unaided; others will benefit from the help of a psychotherapist. In my analysis of how and why people seek psychotherapy, I will explain why so many are disappointed. After exploring this problem, I will offer a prescription for finding the most effective help.

Given the right mix of understanding and courage, midlife adults can exploit a personal crisis to trigger constructive change that enriches the rest of their lives. To do so it is necessary to resist the urge to mask disquieting feelings. Since the transition not only stresses the individual but also shakes the whole family tree, the family will also resist change. The good news is that, just as with individuals, family systems are more capable of changing when they are stirred by a crisis.

As I approached forty, I discovered within myself many of the fears I am describing. This book is part of my own adaptive response to crisis. Writing a book is part counterphobic response—an attempt to master the very thing the author is afraid of—and part an effort to reach out to others. These two themes—conquering inner fears and reaching out to others—are essential elements in overcoming a midlife crisis.

Much of the material for this book is drawn from an analysis of the lives of people in transition. Since many of these people were patients, I have used pseudonyms out of respect for their privacy. I have also learned much about living wisely and well from friends who generously shared their experiences of midlife with me. All have my thanks.

Finally, I would like to thank my editor, Carol Houck Smith, who helped broaden my perspective and challenged me to make this a book that describes the experience and serves the needs of women as well as men.

Michael P. Nichols
Albany, New York

TURNING
FORTY
IN THE
EIGHTIES

1

The Midlife Crisis

SOMEWHERE around the age of forty many men and women suffer a profound personal crisis. For some, the routine of everyday life builds to boredom and despair, for which they anxiously seek reasons and from which they search for escape. For others, life slides by unnoticed until some rash act or unexpected setback—an affair or a promotion that falls through—forces them to recognize that something is dreadfully wrong. In the first case, the reaction is confusion and paralysis; in the second, impulsive action often forces personal change at great cost to family, and ultimately individual, stability and security.

Now at least we have a label for the problem; instead of a nameless and private malady, it has become a recognizable syndrome: the *midlife crisis*. Recently this phenomenon has received a great deal of sympathetic attention. A number of scholarly as well as popular writers have described the common problems of midlife, and most of us now know what to expect, even if we don't know exactly what to do about it.

Most people speed through early adulthood too fixed on external challenges to take a hard look at themselves. These years are not without searching, but the search is directed outward—toward starting a career, getting married, buying a house, and having children. Then one day, somewhere around forty, they stop to ask, "What do I *want,* now that I've done what I was supposed to do?"

Turning forty is like having a bad case of spring fever. The symptoms are familiar—a feeling of stagnation, disequilibrium, and mild depression. Life itself can sap the spirit, just as a long season of winter wears us out, leaving us languid and closed in, longing for the sunshine of spring. Midlife can be a time of wistful yearning, only now the sensation of languor is mixed with regret and the longing for rejuvenation takes on greater urgency. Midlife malaise takes many forms. The most common reaction may be daydreaming of change, whether it be travel, romance, or the success that seems to have eluded us. Various objects of desire embody our fantasies of breaking out.

The daydreams of midlife are filled with images of escape and new beginnings. Unhappy people who feel stuck and stagnant dream of starting over, perhaps somewhere else . . . perhaps *with* someone else. These tantalizing images take whatever shape our frustrated longings dictate; they are as free as the clouds from earthbound constraints. Still, after such flights of fancy, we usually have to come back down to earth.

While the daydreams of spring fever are a reaction to being cooped up all winter, the daydreaming of a discontented forty-year-old results from the sensation of being trapped in a life structure that now feels narrow and restrictive. Young adults, no matter how rigidly their lives are structured, cling to the illusion of unlimited options. Commitments made in the twenties usually have a provisional quality; the future still seems wide open. Choices made may shape the entire course of life, but they don't *feel* permanent and binding. Even a tireless worker or devoted parent may still feel like a youngster, who can always move on if things don't work out. As the years go by, options diminish or vanish. Whether a person feels stuck in a dreary job or an unrewarding marriage, time alone makes it progressively harder to make changes. When dissatisfaction is high and freedom is low, we begin to feel like trapped animals. The full realization of being boxed in is usually slow in coming. To acknowledge openly that our lives aren't working out as planned is threatening, especially if we are afraid to change.

Initially, the feeling of discontent may be vague; it's hard to put a finger on the problem. For this very reason, many people dismiss what they are feeling as unimportant. Those who share their concern with a spouse or friend may be chided for being preoccupied with themselves or teased about having a "midlife crisis," meaning a bit of self-indulgence.

For others, the discontent is more specific and may be focused on a stagnant career, a joyless marriage, or the feeling that physical powers are declining. Often the focus of discontent will be on whatever aspect of life has been overdeveloped. The professional who showed such promise at thirty may feel stuck at a career plateau. The businessman who still thinks of himself as captain of the football team may see the first signs of age in his inability to play more than two sets of tennis or in his spreading waistline. A woman who submerged herself in marriage and childrearing may regret that she sacrificed the opportunity to develop other interests. The woman who put off marriage to concentrate on career may realize she is missing out on the joys of family life.

Growing older is often harder for women in our culture.

Women have a different biological relation to aging. Approaching forty means that the childbearing period is coming to an end—for women, not for men—and many women experience an intense "baby hunger" between the ages of thirty-five and forty. Other women of this age are looking hard for the right partner. Some of them are divorced or widowed; many are raising children on their own; others, who immersed themselves in careers during their twenties and thirties, are finding that the promise of "having it all" was overly optimistic.

Most of us, men and women alike, are vain, though the prospect of aging shocks our vanity in different ways. Men, as they get older, may lose their trim physique and have doubts about their prowess (athletic and sexual). Women, in our youth-oriented culture, may feel that their very sense of worth and desirability is at stake. This may be neither fair nor rational, and attitudes are changing, but women's dreams—for themselves and about themselves—continue to be shaped by masculine perceptions. As a man reaches middle age, he is said to become "mature" or "distinguished"; when a woman gets older, she's likely to be considered, well, "older." Women are twice cursed: when people say, "She must have been pretty when she was younger," they suggest that being pretty is what counts and that youthful attractiveness counts the most.

The Lost Prerogatives of Youth

When we reach our late thirties, we are near the midpoint of life. No gong rings, of course, but twinges begin. A feeling of unease sets in with the realization that this is the end of growing up and the beginning of growing old. Most of us have concluded the preliminary business of adulthood, and now our lives take on a settled quality. This is it, life as a grownup. We look back and see the vitality and endless possibilities of youth; ahead, we see ourselves plodding along well-worn paths, whose shapes were fixed long ago.

Around forty, we become increasingly aware of how many people, not much older than ourselves, are succumbing to heart attacks, cancer, and other diseases. We may live to be eighty, of course, but there are no guarantees. This vision of the future shakes some people badly. Some start to lose heart at the first signs of middle age. This is especially likely to happen to those who cling to the illusion of youth until it can no longer be maintained, whereupon they sink into despair. What makes these people feel even more alone is that midlife is one of the few important life transitions unmarked by a ritual of passage. Baptisms, weddings, retirement parties, and funerals all help us mark change and shift to new ways of relating to each other. None of these events is strictly a function of age, but it is hard to miss them. Developmental transitions in midlife are not strictly a function of age either—some people are just getting married at forty, others are already grandparents—and some people reverse or delay the usual sequence of events. No landmark signals the threshold to maturity, and there are no obvious warnings of crisis. Perhaps that is why there are so many jokes about turning forty; even though nothing really happens on the fortieth birthday, it is a visible symbol of transition and the passage of time.

A woman bursts into tears on her fortieth birthday. Her friends have thrown a surprise party, and she's delighted. There is wine and cake, good friends, and lively conversation. All the people she really cares about are there. She feels loved and appreciated. She doesn't even mind all the jokes about turning forty. Not at first. But then it dawns on her. Here she is, forty years old, and she still hasn't made her mark. She feels she is good enough to have done something special, and she hasn't. The trouble is she can no longer tell herself that she is still a kid and has plenty of time.

Two prerogatives of youth, being promising and being supported, are lost in midlife. The person who is valued at twenty-five for having great potential is expected someday to deliver. By midlife, being promising is no longer enough.

The continuing need for emotional support may be less apparent. After all, the average person prepares to leave home somewhere around eighteen, and by the mid-twenties many people have children of their own. Others, who remain single or do not have children, are equally likely to consider themselves emancipated once they begin paying their own way. Still the feelings of dependency continue, as does the need for support. As long as their parents are alive, most people continue to think of them as potential sources of support. This is true whether or not the parents actually provide real comfort. Some people are fortunate enough to have parents who continue to be a source of wise counsel for many years. The relationship may have switched from parent-child to something like friendship, but the parent is still the older friend. Even when the parents are physically helpless or dependent themselves, most middle-aged children continue to think they *should* be able to count on their parents. Some long actively for the missing nurturance, others simply get angry; both groups, however, are likely to seek substitute parent figures in older colleagues, in friends, in spouses, and sometimes in their own children.

The actual death of a parent is, of course, a clear and dramatic sign that a person is no longer a child and is now truly on his or her own. Freud said that the death of his father was "like being torn up by the roots." Death is final, but at least it is clear. Traumatic as it may be, the bereaved can recognize their loss. Other people can too, and so death and the rituals attending it are unmistakable signs of changing status and the need for special consideration. But most people in midlife have to deal with the loss of parentlike support as a slow accretion of changed responsibility. Because there are few concrete markers of the change, the reasons for the resulting disequilibrium are often unrecognized. For one thing, most people have to deal with the possibility of their parents' death long before the physical fact. Sickness or retirement brings intimations of our parents' mortality, and with it the realization that we are on our own.

Even when parents remain alive and healthy, they may no longer want to *act* like parents to their grown children. Once again, the emotional disruption is insidious, because the change is gradual and vague. Although the source may not be apparent, the result is likely to be a progressive unsettling feeling of being rootless and alone. Often the impact is increased by a parallel process at work. At the same time they are losing dependency on their parents, many people are also losing their junior status at work.

We can all remember being in a hurry to grow up. Growing up meant being in control and doing what we wanted. Once the world seemed divided into two groups: children and grownups. Later, however, we discovered another division: that between juniors and seniors. Juniors are novices, trainees, and assistants; seniors are experts, supervisors, and chiefs. Young workers are often impatient with their long period of apprenticeship and subordinate status. They long for the privileges of rank and power. What they usually don't recognize are the prerogatives of being a junior.

Junior status bestows support and room to maneuver. As in the family, novices can usually turn to older co-workers, like big brothers and sisters, for advice and assistance. No one is particularly threatened by beginners, and so colleagues are happy to help them along. Supervisors and bosses are generally willing to serve as parent figures for younger employees, giving them time and latitude for mistakes in exchange for respect and loyalty.

After a few years, we begin to acquire some of the privileges of rank. It feels good. The boss shows respect, and fellow workers come around for advice. But the other side of the coin is that we are no longer able to lean on older associates for support. Senior colleagues cease deferring to us as juniors—we are one of them. The boss now expects more from us and may even feel threatened and become a rival instead of a sponsor.

When Cathy became a department head at age thirty-six, the men she worked with no longer seemed as friendly. Once they went out of their way to recognize and support her talent. But when she was promoted from executive secretary to administrator, they stopped thinking of her as "clever" and started thinking of her as a rival for the next promotion. She discovered how hard it is for most men to relate to women as competitive equals. The personnel director even suggested that she change from dresses to more masculine attire.

When does all this happen? It doesn't exactly happen, at least not as an event that can be located in time. Growing older and changing status are slow and subtle processes. This is one of the most difficult aspects of midlife anxiety. That is why the discontent is so hard to understand and so hard to talk about.

The Roots of Crisis

What exactly brings about a midlife crisis? Most people do not focus their apprehension on a specific idea. Instead, they have a growing feeling of being caught in a life that is empty, dull, and flat. The feeling is vague; it comes and goes; and the content shifts. There is a sense that youth is running out. Images of aging and death invade waking thoughts. Dreams of young adulthood are discovered to be elusive—or worse, meaningless. It's easy to assume that the images of decline are the cause of the problem. This natural human tendency to accept the content of our fears as their cause is also at work when parents leave the lights on in their children's bedrooms "so that there will be nothing to be afraid of." The embodiment of midlife anxieties as fears of physical decline and death has led some to postulate these as the root of the problem.

Elliot Jaques, a psychoanalyst who studied the lives of 310 creative individuals, stated plainly that the midlife crisis is due to an awareness of the inevitability of death. Finding a marked tendency for a personal crisis to occur in the middle and late thirties, he wrote, "The paradox is that of entering the prime of life, the stage of fulfillment, but at the same time the prime and fulfillment are dated. Death lies beyond." Other writers, notably Ernest Becker, Norman O. Brown, and Robert Jay Lifton have agreed. We have two great fears: fear of life and fear of death. The fear of death becomes more prominent in midlife.

Another nominee for *the* cause of the midlife crisis is biological. According to this line of thinking, the emotional upheavals of midlife are stimulated by hormonal changes—in women, by the onset of menopause; in men, by the climacteric.

Menopause is a complex phenomenon, with enough lack of information to allow free play for our biases. Doctors who do not understand the physiology of hormonal changes often tell women patients that their menopausal distress is neurotic—depriving these women of dignity *and* hormone replacement therapy. At other times, women are told that whatever they are feeling is due entirely to their hormones. In this way, unhappiness, loneliness, and legitimate complaints are consigned to the status of biological side effects—and thus invalidated.

Menopausal problems are real and directly related to physiological changes. Researchers have found a clear-cut and simple correspondence between hormone levels and distress. As many as 85 percent of women may experience hot flashes, night sweats, and insomnia. What is less clear is how many women suffer significant emotional upset along with these physical symptoms. But men and women both experience glandular changes too late in life to explain the crisis at age forty. Although some worry about it, most women do not encounter the first changes in their menstrual cycles until their mid-forties and do not reach menopause until about age fifty. Men do not undergo a shift in testosterone levels until they reach the late forties or early fifties. Moreover, there is mounting evidence that the psychological effects of hormonal fluctuations are minimal.

That biological explanations for problems in living remain popular is a tribute to the human wish for simple solutions to complex problems. This particular one—menopause as the cause of midlife crisis (only recently extended to men in the form of "male menopause")—is a lingering form of sexism, according to which women are thought to be slaves to their bodies and therefore not capable of full participation in human affairs.

Tempting as single-factor explanations are, there is no single cause of the midlife crisis. The fact that the crisis lacks a clear-cut precipitant is evidence that it is based on something in the person, not in the environment. But the something in the person is more than hormones. The danger of overemphasizing biology is the danger of neglecting problems in living *and* of avoiding the responsibility to change behavior that isn't working. There are too many psychological factors involved to credit exclusively biological explanations.

Midlife shocks in the exterior world lead to a crisis when they jar loose interior anxieties. Loss or even change of jobs, separation, divorce—these shocks do not *cause* the crisis, but the fact that they involve conflicting choices and blows to self-esteem is a clue to its nature.

We should recognize that not everyone has a midlife crisis. Some people remain stable and their lives continue as before. One estimate of this number comes from Daniel Levinson, in his book *The Seasons of a Man's Life*. Levinson found that 80 percent of the men in his study had a tumultuous struggle with themselves and their environment at about age forty; that leaves 20 percent who apparently suffered no crisis. What are the comparable figures for women? Unfortunately, we don't know because there are as yet no similar studies made of women. My guess is that women have as many problems as men but, because women's lives are more complicated with multiple role demands, their crises are more variable than men's.

What can those people who pass smoothly from their thirties to their forties and beyond teach us? I have met and interviewed several such people and found that they worked out relatively satisfactory life structures early in their adult years *and* made minor readjustments along the way. Some people make changes in a relatively unself-conscious way. I am not one of these. In my thirties I bumped hard against flaws in my own character that I could not simply overcome with willpower. I have had to work hard to understand myself and to make changes, transforming a negative experience into something positive. Because my own transition was painful and deliberate, I envy those who have made changes gradually and consistently.

Yet the absence of a recognizable midlife crisis can be deceptive. Some people experience a personal disruption with the intensity of a crisis, but since it is nowhere near their fortieth birthday they do not perceive it as a midlife crisis. One person I interviewed said he thought the idea of a midlife crisis was "interesting," but he had not experienced anything like what I was describing. When I asked about his career, he told the following story: At age twenty-nine he had gone to work for United Press hoping to become a foreign correspondent. He worked hard and was eventually promoted to overnight editor. But there he stayed. His superiors felt that his talent was as an editor, that he didn't have the speed or temperament to be a reporter. So he was stalled. Worse, he began to doubt his own worth. He began to think of himself as uncreative, in his words, "a hack." He became depressed, but not enough to seek help; he became alienated from his wife and children, but not enough to cause a breakup. Then, when he was forty-six, he made a major career change, leaving the wire service and going to work for the Voice of America. Here he found the perfect vehicle for his talents, and he became a successful feature writer whose work is admired throughout the Third World.

The midlife crisis usually occurs somewhere in the late thirties, but it is not merely a function of age. The reason it seems to occur in a certain age group is that most men and women get married or start careers, or both, in their early twenties. Whatever form the life structure takes—single person, wife and mother, working mother, father who shares childrearing or not—it usually needs readjustment after ten or fifteen years. People who marry earlier or later, those who divorce, get a late start on a career, or have children when they are very young —in other words, people who erect a preliminary adult life structure at an atypical age—are likely to have a midlife crisis out of sequence. The editor turned feature writer described above experienced a classic midlife crisis out of sequence—in fact, only slightly out of sequence. Starting a career at age twenty-nine is a little late, but given the late start he found it necessary to readjust that part of his life just about on schedule. His midlife crisis was recognizable, but delayed.

The Masked Crisis

Sometimes a crisis in midlife occurs without being recognized, because the symptoms are masked and the causes remain unexamined. Some of these masking reactions are destructive enough to be seen as a problem, but others deaden the pain without removing the source. A gradual increase in nightly drinking, a discreet series of affairs, or an insidious pattern of withdrawal—these corrosive habits are among the common devices for masking the critical need to readjust life at forty. Drinking may lead to alcoholism, affairs may end in divorce, but often in cases of "masked crisis" the crisis subsides without change, the critical point is passed, and the outcome is a stagnant second half of life.

The truth is, the prime of life is not youth but middle age. That is not the issue. The issue is how people interpret the personal meaning of becoming middle-aged. Regardless of what their heads tell them, many people believe in their hearts that they are starting to slip when they approach forty. The idea of a middle-age crisis is frightening, and many people deal with their fears by denying them. Thus the same forces at work in creating the crisis—including the fear of aging—are partly responsible for denying that it exists.

The person I was at thirty would not have accepted what I am writing here at forty. Like many people I was too fixed on what I was doing to consider where I was going. If someone had raised the problems I am raising here, I would have raised my defenses and turned away.

Besides suggesting some failure to cope with the realities of life, the concept of a middle-age crisis lends itself to trivialization. It is often transmitted in such a way that it seems a cliché—and none of us likes to think of ourselves as suffering from a cliché.

Practiced self-deceit, which we sometimes confuse with maturity, makes us uncomfortable with anything that suggests we still have some growing up to do. Convinced that maturity is knowing how to survive, we put our heads down and plow through the business of adult life. Unfortunately, this kind of survival is an art that requires dulling the mind and the senses.

Believing that growing older is the only source of the midlife crisis is a fallacy, based, perhaps, on the secret conviction that getting older is a problem in and of itself. In any case, a substantial number of people think that having a midlife crisis means a self-pitying inability to accept the natural course of aging, as though aging were nothing but an abstract political issue and all right-thinking people accepted it.

The topic of aging makes most people uncomfortable, and their contempt for the idea of a midlife crisis is fueled both by their own resistance and by the excesses of behavior that are part of the stereotyped reaction to middle age. Hooked at an early age on the transient values of youth, some people react to their fortieth birthday with an orgy of self-indulgence. Frightened by the signs of aging, they lose interest in the welfare of others and seek by every means possible to prolong their own youth. There is a social imperative to stay young, but people who are too obvious about doing so become objects of scorn, like the powdered and rouged old gentleman in Thomas Mann's *Death in Venice*. Such figures of ridicule are part of the image conjured up by the label "midlife crisis," but an even stronger reason for rejection is based on denial of the need for change.

Change is hard. Hard at twenty, harder at forty. Besides, no one told us that we would have to readjust our lives in the middle. Just to admit that idea into consciousness is unsettling.

Crisis as Opportunity

For many of us, having a crisis implies failure and weakness, an inability to endure life. This perception stems in part from a failure to distinguish between two separate meanings of *crisis*. The first meaning is developmental: *crisis* as a turning point or an unstable condition in which there is impending change. The second meaning is pathological: *crisis* as a sudden emergency in the course of a disease. We tend to think of unsettling life events in purely negative terms; crisis then seems a foreign body to be gotten rid of, or a problem for the self, rather than *of* the self. And the ideal solution seems to be a return to the status quo.

When I told my friends and colleagues that I was writing a book on the midlife crisis, some responded as though accused: "*I* didn't have any crisis." They might have been less threatened—and more open—if I had said that I was writing a book on depression. Noting this negative reaction to the word crisis, Gail Sheehy substituted a more neutral term, *passages,* when writing about life's critical transition points in her book of that title. Despite the resistance it conjures up, the term "crisis" is most apt because of its double meaning—crisis as both a developmental turning point and a time of acute distress. Not only is the distress a fact of life for many people in midlife transition; it also serves a useful function.

Crisis need not be a calamity; it can be an opportunity. As

people move across time, they experience crisis at critical junctures. These are times of increased vulnerability and heightened potential for growth. Once we understand that our lives include a series of developmental crises, we will no longer think of life as a process of slow and steady growth, or adulthood as a static period. The midlife crisis is one of several disruptions that undermine a person's secure position in the world. The woman or man in midlife crisis is not mentally *de*ranged, but *dis-arranged;* and the disarrangement, for all its pain, has the creative potential to propel the person to break out of a lifestyle that no longer seems to work.

Normally—no, ideally—the developmental issues of midlife are resolved gradually. When this happens we may hardly notice them. A more dramatic crisis occurs when we are confronted with an issue we haven't yet dealt with. It might be an affair that dramatizes the sterility of a marriage, a heart attack that drives home the impermanence of life, or a layoff from work that simultaneously undermines financial security and the illusion of having "made it." These upheavals shake us to our roots, disrupting painfully worked-out roles and redefining the rules. Sometimes, when this happens, a powerful and preoccupying idea takes hold: "There is no one left to take care of me," "I am going to die," or "I am a failure."

Midlife is *not* too late for significant personal change; it only seems that way. The crisis occurs when we are squeezed between inner pressure to change and all that stands in our way. A midlife crisis is painful, but it may provide the necessary shock to disrupt our defenses so that we can reexamine our lives— inside and out. A life without pain is a life without passion.

2

Midlife and the Adult Life Cycle

SOME theorists claim that our basic psychological makeup is laid down in early childhood. But experience teaches that the cycle of life requires growth and change for adults as well as children. If character were permanently set in childhood, there would be no chance for change in midlife.

Various authors have devised ways for analyzing the human life cycle. Most of them introduce a series of stages with appropriate disclaimers of rigid regularity. Daniel Levinson's scheme, worked out on a sample limited to men, includes eleven subphases of adulthood, punctuated by transitional periods. This is the theme of the life-cycle literature: adulthood is a time of many tasks that order the days of our lives. Theodore Lidz defines the stages of adulthood as "The Young Adult," "The Middle Years," "Old Age," and "Death." He avoids specifying particular ages for these periods, but does note that women seem to reach every stage before men do.

Erik Erikson provided the first psychological model of development throughout life, and he popularized the concept of the life cycle. Distinguishing eight stages from birth to maturity, he helped correct the myopic focus on childhood, which had previously characterized studies of human development. Although Erikson devoted three stages to adulthood, his greatest emphasis was on the *identity crisis* of adolescence. Thanks to Erikson, members of the baby boom generation had a lot of attention paid to their teenage identity crises and existential neuroses. There were more of these young people, so we paid more attention to them. The result was an exaggerated celebration of the adolescent rites of passage in the "now generation." Today those same people are reaching middle age—and their problems haven't ceased.

Becoming an Adult

Despite what teenagers think, young men and women do not suddenly become adult at age eighteen, or even twenty-one. The transition from adolescence to adulthood begins in the late teens, but extends until about thirty. At age seventeen, we imagined that when we finished school, moved out of our parents' house, started a career, and got married—events we expected to accomplish by the mid-twenties—we would be full-fledged adults. Looking back, it is easy to see how adolescent we still were throughout our twenties.

By the end of adolescence most people are well on their way to breaking away from their families and defining separate identities. But the process is gradual and protracted. Leaving home and entering the adult world are complementary achievements. A promising start on a career or marriage makes it easier to give up the dependent attachment to one's parents. People who remain psychologically enmeshed with their families may have a harder time grabbing hold of life or may not be able to do so at all. In the usual case, letting go and taking hold proceed in leapfrog fashion, with progress in one sphere reinforcing progress in the other. Going away to college, for example, makes young people feel more secure and adult in relationship to parents, which in turn frees them to become more emotionally involved in new relationships with friends and lovers. Or, as Erik Erikson put it, real intimacy with others is only possible after establishing an independent identity.

Successfully negotiating young adulthood is a balancing act. One begins to build a stable life structure, while at the same time remaining flexible enough to tear down and rebuild elements that prove unsatisfactory. There is no single standard for a satisfactory style of life; a life structure is functional if it is viable in society and true to the self. Once, the traditional family—made up of a wage-earning father, an economically and socially dependent mother, and two or more children—was so common as to be nearly universal. But in the 1980s this is no longer true. Alternative lifestyles have become increasingly prevalent, complicating the choices of early adulthood. Marriage and family (or cohabitation, or remaining unattached), work, residence, style of life, friendships, leisure activities, religion, and involvement in community life—these are the components of a life structure. A full life is balanced, but when we are young we concentrate on what seems most essential. Few of us can dedicate time and energy to more than one or two of these components—three at the most. One of the great frustrations in life is thinking about all the interests there is no time for; but doing some things well means not trying to do everything.

Freud said love and work are the primary routes to mature satisfaction. For men, this may be an effective formula for the good life; for women it often entails a painful choice. Many people center their lives around marriage/family and a career, usually changing the relative investment of energy from one to the other as time goes by. That is another hard lesson about the choices in life: you do not simply make choices and be done with it; you have to renew and deepen some commitments, while relaxing or abandoning others.

Sometimes we can identify trouble spots by noting which of the basic goals of young adulthood have not been achieved. Not everyone gets married, and not all of those who do marry do so in their twenties. Nevertheless, people have to make choices and then try to bring them to fruition. Failure to complete any of the component tasks of young adulthood is due either to a more or less deliberate choice or to some kind of personal failure.

One person may choose to delay marriage in order to get established in a career; another may want to get married but cannot find the right person or perhaps has trouble sustaining an intimate relationship. Whether it is due to intentional decision or merely to the cards that life deals, the preliminary life structure worked out in the twenties may need to be modified in the thirties. Every positive choice has a negative counterpart. Some parts of the self are inevitably neglected or suppressed. For a woman, the pursuit of further education may mean not being able to stay at home with small children. Settling down also has its price, restricting the freedom to wander and explore. Women who choose a family over a career may unnecessarily limit future options. The opposite can happen too, and some women who put their careers ahead of everything else discover in midlife that something vital is missing. Men who neglect their children in order to get ahead may rob themselves and their children of an irreplaceable experience. Every road taken in the twenties limits the pathways still open in the forties.

Like all living things, human beings seek stability and security. In fact, most of our efforts in the first half of life are directed toward achieving and maintaining stability. Young adulthood is a time of opportunity and a time of stress. Both factors make people want to settle down. The greater the opportunity or the stress, the greater the likelihood of settling prematurely into a constricted structure. We all know people who married in a rush in order to escape their unhappy homes, and many of us look back with regret that we broke off our training to take what looked like a golden opportunity.

The early years of marriage and childrearing are enormously trying. The cultural myth of getting married and "living happily ever after" leaves most people unprepared for the painful period of accommodation required to get from the wedding ceremony to a marriage of separate lives. Babies—those cute little creatures who smile at us in television commercials— bring sleepless nights and a revisitation of painful family conflicts. The unfinished battles with our parents now have to be fought all over again with our spouses and children. These battles—indeed many of the struggles of early adulthood— leave little time for reevaluation or readjustment. Because young adults are so busy getting there, they have less time to think about where they are going. The twenties and thirties may be the most stressful period of life, but young adults, with full physical and emotional vigor, can still make major changes. The variability is, of course, enormous: some people move steadily and smoothly through the early years of adulthood; others cling tenaciously to bad marriages or jobs with little future. Most people, however, continue to follow a life-cycle pattern with alternating periods of growth and stability. The typical path of human development is similar to Thomas Kuhn's version of the growth of science: spasms of paradigmatic change, with periods of consolidation and stability in between. Following the hard choices of transition, a number of preferred ways of handling problems are developed, both for the puzzles of normal science and for everyday demands of love and work.

Men's Lives, Women's Lives

Most authors of the life-cycle literature are men, and most of the studies have been done on men. These men, writing about men, acknowledge that women are different, but are hard-pressed to say how. When I began to write this book, I hoped to minimize distinctions between men and women. My idea was to describe the midlife crisis as it affects various "people," each of whom may be different but all of whom share themes. It didn't work. Every person's story is different; there are common themes, but it isn't possible to write about people as though men and women were (basically) the same. They aren't. It isn't so much that women have different tasks in their progress through life, but that today their life cycles are so much more variable and complex.

The overwhelming priority of work constricts and simplifies men's lives. Most young men concentrate on their careers until sometime after midlife when they shift to a greater investment in their families and private lives. Women's lives, on the other hand, are complicated by multiple roles and multiple sequences. Many women marry and raise children in their twenties, and then return to work sometime in their thirties. But there are now so many alternative courses of development that it is no longer possible to speak of this as the average pattern. The point is not that men and women have totally separate concerns, but that a modern woman's passage through the life cycle is complicated by a greater number of options and more pressure about timing. Men may father children in young adulthood or later in middle age; women are limited to their years of fertility, and most women do not want to risk bearing children over the age of forty. Moreover, once they do have children, most women are tied to them, at least until the children are ready for school. If you calculate the possible combinations of marrying or not, having children or not, having children earlier or later, working or not, and working part- or full-time, you will see the enormous number of choices faced by women today.

Whether the transition to midlife is smooth or turbulent, there is bound to be some disillusionment. Long-held assumptions are challenged in an often painful process during which the person modifies the illusions and the life structure of early adulthood. The result is a sense of loss and liberation—loss of sustaining beliefs and cherished hopes—but there is also an increased freedom to be what you are and can be. No longer pursuing an idealized dream based on a childhood script, the midlife adult can begin to live a full life within the bounds of what is real—about the world and about the self.

In midlife there is a modest decline in the elemental drives and a gradual diminution of physical powers. Even little changes can be maddening. Being unable to read street signs without glasses, losing names in memory's overloaded grooves, or suffering the protest of aching muscles after vigorous exercise—these are among the annoying signals that you aren't the person you used to be. The bad news—that it is time to give up certain youthful activities—is especially distressing to those people who retain childhood images of youth and age.

Our image of old age doesn't fit the facts. Advances in health care—and more important, in understanding—have made life longer and better. Yet as we enter middle adulthood most of us contemplate a future shaped by images we grew up with. The image of old people as feeble and childish may be false, but, lodged deep in our minds, it is a very real fear.

Youth and age are archetypal symbols, pregnant with meaning. "Youth" means budding, growing, full of promise, and vigorous. "Old" means stagnant, feeble, weak, obsolete, sick, and dying. This may not be the full picture in our rational minds, but these are the images of interior anxiety jarred loose by the shock of reaching middle age. Normally, we also begin to realize that getting older means maturity, better judgment, self-awareness, experience, and mellowness. Although we may think of life as half over at forty, many of us still have half our lives to live. What we fear—middle age—is, in fact, filled with opportunity.

A friend of mine writes: "Would you like to know how I feel about middle age? I find myself mellowing with maturity, more willing to "let it be," and less prone to authority hassles. I like being a big shot at work, which means more money and more respect. It seems to help the mellowness. I less often see women on the street that "I have to have," and I have more fun and love in bed than before. On the negative side, I don't like getting fatter in the middle and thinner on top. All in all, it's not a bad trade. I seem to have come to terms with my life. I like being forty-seven."

Successful transition to midlife means keeping what is youthful in oneself, while accepting what is older. In practice this means scaling down some ambitions, accepting certain limits, but also becoming reinvigorated by reclaiming qualities that were denied in young adulthood.

In order to make their way in the world, men and women of the postwar generation typically concentrated on a limited range of their potential talents—those that they considered their strengths—which, by the way, often turned out to be related to sex-role stereotypes. Young men developed their "masculine" side; they were tough, aggressive, and hard-driving; they tackled the world of work. Young women tended to rely on what they were taught were their feminine qualities; they were soft, tender, and maternal; they made homes and had babies. These gender-linked stereotypes were further polarized in the complementary marriage, which was still the standard only a few years ago. Young married partners formed a yoked team. Together they equalled a whole person; separately each was one-dimensional and incomplete. Now, in midlife, it is possible to achieve a more balanced integration.

Meaning and Satisfaction

Many people pass through their thirties like sleepwalkers, chasing dreams whose unconscious motives and conflicts they hardly suspect. Exhausted by the responsibility of trying to get ahead, they long to shuck off responsibility altogether. Some do. They leave duty and responsibility behind and set off with the wind of the world in their faces. Thanks to "women's liberation" this is more possible than ever for men. Women are now officially no longer helpless; men are not required to take care of them. Legal obligations and moral penalties for divorce are now considerably relaxed. This should make everything equal, right? Wrong. Women who take advantage of the new morality to leave their husbands run smack up against the hard reality that sex discrimination hasn't changed much in the world of work. Moreover, women who have sacrificed their own self-development to raise families don't return to the job market with equal credentials. If she is left with the kids, a woman's difficulty doubles. Divorce precipitates at least two crises. In addition to the obvious physical disruption, the partner who leaves is liable to reap a bitter harvest of conflict and guilt; the one who is left behind often suffers a critical loss of self-esteem.

Maybe most middle-aged people think about flying the

coop, but most don't do it. Instead, the majority scale down their professional aspirations and become more involved with their families. This common pattern is endorsed by most of the experts on midlife. Wise men and women, we are told by Gail Sheehy, find serenity in the second half of life by "letting go of the impossible dream, and discovering the joys of caring." Daniel Levinson says that in midlife "internal voices that have been muted for years now clamor to be heard." Finally one can now "listen more attentively to these voices and decide consciously what part he will give them in his life." The trouble with this formula for authenticity is that it underestimates unconscious imperatives and overestimates the individual's ability to decide his or her fate. Aging does not insure maturity.

Not all of us are in command of the decisions that shape our lives; not everyone realizes that he or she is unhappy before suddenly making a change. Some changes are the result of adjustment to circumstances—physical, financial, or familial. Turning forty in "an age of diminishing expectations" makes it even harder to accept limitations in the self. In addition, many seemingly deliberate choices reflect family pressure far more than is apparent. When mothers return to work in middle age they do so for a variety of good reasons: to earn more money, to escape the boredom of living in a world of children, to express their creative urges, to exercise skills and talents, or just to get out of the house. Most women also get a good deal of subtle and not so subtle pressure from their husbands to work or develop other outside interests.

Men and women apparently do not develop synchronously or at the same rate, but the pressures they exert on each other for changes in midlife are often complementary. He wants her to return to work to earn more money, but also to continue shouldering the major share of childrearing. She wants him to "realize his full potential" (incidentally earning more money), or to develop the softer side of himself and share the joys of taking care of the children—or both.

One of the outcomes of the midlife transition is supposed to be concern for and involvement with other people, especially children and younger colleagues. Erikson's term for this accomplishment is "generativity," and it comes highly recommended by all the experts on midlife. As a matter of fact, generativity is a good thing—or should be. Loving concern for other people is a natural urge in a fulfilled person. Alfred Adler recognized this and equated "social interest" with mental health. Generativity as defined here does not necessarily mean becoming a parent. It means assuming parental responsibility in a creative new sense as guide and mentor to younger adults. Generativity is not unique to middle age, but it is of special relevance to the midlife transition. In people who achieved a feeling of well-being through personal accomplishment, generativity is—as it is claimed to be—one of the culminating expressions of maturity. People who have fought their way to success can now find additional satisfaction in helping others along the same path. Others, who have not reached their goals, may turn to helping roles as a defensive compensation for personal failure. For these people the shift to generativity is a shift to finding gratification through alter egos, not a noble or generous impulse.

Loving people means loving them as they are; to the extent that you love them you do not need them to change. There is nothing wrong or ignoble about wanting someone to change, but the truth is that wanting someone to change is motivated by some personal need. When we pressure our single friends to get married, our divorced friends to remarry, or childless couples to have babies, we are projecting our own internal standard of what it means to be grown up. Other times, we do just the opposite and, in the name of being helpful, encourage our friends to act out our own dissatisfactions.

There are two problems with the concept of generativity, both of which are endemic to the life-cycle literature as a whole. The first is a consequence of linear thinking; the second is a result of the male bias in the literature. Erikson's eight stages of ego development—the inspiration of the life-cycle literature—portray human nature as a sort of linear development, ever onward, ever upward. A truer picture of human development is a spiral; earlier stages are never transcended, tasks are never completed. Developmental challenges are not passed or failed, but dealt with more or less effectively, and we don't leave them behind; they recede in importance.

If "spiral" is the more apt term, why have I retained the standard phrase "life cycle"? Cycles refer to the repeating sequences, like summer, fall, winter, and spring, that are the rhythms of nature. "Life cycle" remains the best choice to describe human development, because the development of human life is repeated from one generation to the next. The individual's life span is part of the family's life cycle. Later, I will explain how it is impossible to understand individual development fully without keeping in mind the family context.

The second problem with the concept of generativity is that it is probably more important for the development of men than of women. Most men spend their early adult years trying to make a living and trying to succeed. Middle age, for many men, is a plateau, a level of sufficient success to satisfy some of their economic and psychological needs. They may go on to higher levels of achievement, but now they have adequate security to become less selfish and more concerned for others. But what about women? From an early age, women in our culture are taught to dedicate their whole lives to generativity. Little girls are supposed to play with dolls; young women are supposed to take care of babies. For the many women who do devote their twenties and thirties to taking care of children, midlife may be more appropriately a time to develop healthy self-interest than generativity.

The Fear of Old Age

Erikson's eighth and final stage of ego development is *integrity versus despair*. Looking back over a life well-lived produces an inner peace and a conviction of personal significance. Integrity comes from accepting life as it was—and is—without undue regret or recrimination. Those who cannot accept the past, or the present, fall into despair; they are filled with self-hatred and bitterness toward others. Unfortunately, many people anticipate despair and bitterness as inevitable in late adulthood.

Today there is a renewed interest in and show of respect toward elderly people in our country. That such a readjustment was needed in the first place shows how much we misunderstand and fear old age. But how real is our acceptance of aging when we sugarcoat the reality of the elderly by calling them "senior citizens" or "golden agers"? And why do we laugh when old people in situation comedies defy conventions of gentility by cracking dirty jokes, or otherwise behaving in a vulgar manner? This is a cheap form of black humor in which the audience is invited to discharge emotional tension about something that causes fear.

Death is the ultimate fear, and now it draws near. The idea that we will one day become food for worms is impossible to conceive in childhood, easy to forget in middle age, but hard to escape in old age. Not that anyone lets the full weight of this sink in, at least not for long. But death anxiety is there in the background, haunting our dreams, and changing the significance of what we do with our remaining time.

A common joke about getting old is that it is better than the alternative. The point seems to be that although they are alive, old people have nothing to celebrate. The joke is a telling admission of just how frightened most of us are of growing old. There may be many reasons for this fear—fear of dying, dread of the unknown, the conditioning of a youth-centered culture—but at its heart are two fundamental problems that are the major themes of this book: mortal fear of weakness and the apparent conflict between individual fulfillment and loving family bonds. Our relationship to these two problems plays a large part in determining how we face old age. Those who can neither admit weakness nor accept their place in a system larger than themselves struggle vainly against the effects of aging. Those who are willing to yield power and influence, allow the center of gravity to shift beyond themselves, and accept a less dominant position in society are free to enjoy a productive and happy late adulthood.

Continuity in Change

What can we conclude from studies of the life cycle? The main point is that there is a rhythm to growth; each of us is unique, but similar. By laying out the universal struggles that define the human condition, the life-cycle literature brings order and continuity to events that otherwise seem to alternate between chaos and stagnation. We progress in stages with plateaus and developmental crises that demand change. The good news is that growth is not one long uphill struggle. We reach plateaus and can coast. The bad news is that we can't stay forever in one place—twenty-one is not the top of the hill. Adulthood used to be thought of as a lengthy stable phase of life, and the adult as a finished product. As we have seen, however, adults continue to evolve through a series of stages; developmental tasks are never fully solved and new ones continue to emerge.

Heraclitus, an Ionian Greek who lived in the sixth and fifth centuries B.C., said that change is the ultimate nature of reality. Nothing is permanent; flux alone is real. Most of us are familiar with his famous epigram: "No one can step into the same river twice." Like all things, water is forever flowing. (He might have added that, like the river, a person is never the same from one moment to the next.) Today, Heraclitus' position sounds very modern. It is in tune with the latest principles of physics and psychology. He abandoned the concept of basic "stuff" and substituted the concept of process—not just change but ordered change.

Life *is* change; it is a process, not a product. The same is true in the life of a great city. Streets under repair, old buildings being torn down and replaced—change—*that* is permanent, not the configuration of streets and buildings at any one time.

The cycle of human life may be orderly, but it is not a steady, continuous process. Periods of growth and change are followed by periods of relative stability in which changes are consolidated. In between these plateaus of constancy are transitional periods, more or less wrenching, depending upon the strength of personal resources and the flexibility of the social context. These are moments of crisis when the basis of personal security and satisfaction is in jeopardy. Too much change threatens security, too little results in stagnation. Like snails, people must periodically shed their shells in order to expand.

Successful adaptation to midlife may require significant changes—in occupation, family, leisure, friendships, health habits, and other important aspects of life. But change is hard, and the human mind is stubborn. So people everywhere resist change or get stuck in the process. Furthermore, the most important changes are not only, or even necessarily, external. The real change is internal—in our attitudes and dreams—and interpersonal—in our mode of relating to others.

People are certainly capable of solving their own problems. In fact, most of us usually do so long before the problems reach crisis proportions. But once a crisis develops, we often get stuck, using more of the same strategies that led to the difficulty in the first place. An equally unfortunate human propensity is to apply solutions where there is no problem. Trying to fix "the generation gap" is an example. Members of the species *psychotherapist* are especially prone to seek cures where there is no disease. Disruption, dis-ease, and self-questioning, though common in midlife, are not universal. Some people don't have a crisis. But for every one of these, there are several who have a crisis out of sequence or who mistake a developmental crisis for something else altogether. Most of us react automatically to anxiety. Rather than containing such feelings long enough to figure out what they are about, we act to dispel the first feelings of disquiet.

Our insides—our very selves—are foreign to us. Self-imposed limitations of perception and imagination seem to make it easier to keep us at the practical business of living. Young adults leave behind the soul-searching of adolescence. Intent on automatic and uncritical living—what the existentialists called "inauthentic"—they set their sights firmly on the exterior landscape. In midlife, the discovery of unresolved interior dilemmas—the realization that life is not as we pretended it was—seems an unacceptable form of weakness.

Hostility toward the midlife crisis, another syndrome of human weakness, is a hostility toward admitting one's own insecurity and toward considering reorganizing a painstakingly constructed life structure. We live by lying to ourselves about our selves. The hostility is defensive. We protect ourselves by avoiding full consciousness of unpleasant or dangerous truths.

The second half of life is more than simply an elaboration of the first. Age forty is, in Jung's words, "the noon of life," when a person's powers reach their zenith and he or she has the opportunity to develop and integrate previously neglected aspects of the total personality. People who speed through young adulthood rigid and uptight have the chance, in maturity, to uncover hidden potential for self-fulfillment.

3

Turning Forty in the Eighties

THE difficulty of leaving youth behind is an abiding human problem, but turning forty is a little different for each generation. Conditions of modern culture have made it harder, not easier. At the same time as the structure of our lives is being undermined by doubts from within, our society is undergoing radical transformations. In a world where the ground is shifting around us, it is doubly hard to find our bearings.

Those of us entering midlife in the eighties were born in an era of orderly prosperity. The children of the 1950s thought that things would stay pretty much the same as they grew up. Yearly changes in the design of automobiles and a steady stream of new popular songs did not alter the perception that the world would not change much. Today the threats of nuclear annihilation, dwindling natural resources, and ecological disaster have given concrete substance to the nightmare that the world might end.

The list of social and technological changes in the lifetime of people turning forty in the 1980s is a long one. Some of these —television, jet travel, even desegregation—have been a part of our cultural experience too long to complicate the midlife passage. The Vietnam War has come and gone. While half a generation marched in battle, the other half marched in protest. And for the first time, many people did both. The war, and the fact that we lost it, caused widespread disillusion, bitterness, and a turning inward. The war convulsed our youth, but its influence is already a part of us.

Some significant occurrences and discoveries mark our history but do not shape our lives. We wept when John F. Kennedy was assassinated and cheered when artificial heart recipient Barney Clark took his first steps; but then we went about our business. Other undeniably dramatic events, like the exploration of space, may affect the lives of our children, but they do not as yet affect us. Eliminating from consideration those events that have already changed our lives, as well as those that have yet to do so, leaves some things that are currently transforming the world of everyday experience, making it quite different from the world of our early adult years. Economic decline, changing sex roles, and the computer revolution— these things are happening now.

Struggling to Make It

Human affairs are always and profoundly influenced by economic conditions, theorists from Marx to Keynes tell us. If this is true, what is so unique about the impact of the current economy? Why is it necessary to include a section on the economy to explain today's midlife crisis? Part of the answer lies in economic conditions themselves. Inflation, recession, and unemployment have created personal crises for thousands of men and women and exacerbated existing problems for thousands more. If we look beyond this general strain, however, we can see that the recent course of the American economy has deteriorated in a way that particularly frustrates the hopes and expectations of those reaching midlife in the 1980s.

One of the great themes of adult life is struggling hard to make it; pausing in midlife to reassess the meaning of life and readjust one's values accordingly; and then, in maturity, discovering the satisfaction of nonmaterial pursuits. This pattern recurs so often in studies of the adult life cycle that it seems universal. In the background of these studies were economic conditions so constant that their influence went unnoticed. Virtually every one of the well-known studies of adult development used male samples born between 1920 and the end of the Great Depression. This was a small cohort (the birthrate was low), and these men grew to maturity in an ever-expanding economy. Just the opposite is true for women and men turning forty in the 1980s.

The high birthrate following World War II created a large cohort—the baby boom generation—overloading the capacity of our economic and social institutions. Fields with constant or shrinking numbers of jobs were pressed by a large group of job seekers. This was especially true for careers in child care and education, when the birthrate declined in the sixties and seventies. College faculty is a striking example, as a generation of scholars completed their doctorates only to find that academic openings had largely evaporated. Now many of them are making due with compromise careers.

By and large, the generation reared in the unprecedented prosperity of the 1950s turned twenty in the 1960s unconcerned with material values. The relative affluence of their parents and the prospect of more of the same for themselves was the background context that enabled them to question traditional values, including the work ethic. Then the economy played a cruel trick. In their thirties, as this group was settling down, they accepted denial and postponement as the inevitable prelude to enjoying a comfortable middle age. They were conditioned to expect to live on less in advanced age, but the steady erosion of spending power in their peak earning years came as a harsh and unexpected blow.

Today's forty-year-olds cannot be unaware of the impact of the economy on their lives. As widespread reporting of the economy moved it from a background influence to a blunt reality of experience, it became more and more difficult to turn away from material values. It's hard to forget financial worries when the morning paper and evening news constantly remind us about rising interests rates and the shrinking value of the dollar. Decline, and our awareness of it, has resulted in money dominating our lives and preoccupying our minds.

A study of the effects of inflation on family stress found that inflation is almost universally depressing. Sixty-seven percent of the families studied experienced moderate to high stress due to inflation. The larger the family the greater the strain. Families respond to the pinch by cutting back on luxuries and entertainment—precisely what most middle-class Americans have learned to rely on for the relief of stress. As they are forced to stay at home more, many families are further stressed by unaccustomed proximity.

According to the Department of Commerce, Bureau of the Census, the median family income in 1960 was $5,620; in 1970 it was $9,867, and in 1980 it was $21,023. Many forty-year-old adults are earning more than they ever dreamed of, but most of them are living less well than they expected. Anticipating the prime of life, they found their savings eaten away by a corrosive cycle of inflation and recession. Loss of their reserves magnified the difficulty of adjusting to shrinking possibilities in later years. No matter what they once thought or still hope for, most midlife adults now realize that the only way they'll ever be well-off is to hit the lottery.

Added to the financial burdens are the monumental weight of children's college expenses, actual or anticipated. Just as many couples have adjusted to "life after children," they are encountering another unexpected form of economic fallout. Because of the unhospitable economy, some grown children return to live at home after graduation from college. Even those who strike out on their own may not be able to make it without help from their parents. This "unempty nest syndrome" puts a tremendous strain on parents who were getting used to living for themselves and children who were looking forward to full emancipation.

While economists and politicians nervously debate causes and cures of failed economic policy, the rest of us are left to deal with the effects. The most visible and significant sign of recession has been a steady increase in unemployment.

The impact of unemployment falls heavily on the families of people who lose their jobs. Their problems are vital and elemental, but at least they are tangible. Human nature is such that we cope better with burdens that are clear and concrete than with unseen or vague threats to our well-being. Unemployment actually strikes less than 10 percent of the population, but it hangs like a threat over us all.

As we've seen, a chief cause of the midlife crisis is the feeling of being frozen into a life structure that no longer appears to work. Recognizing the constraint, many people make adjustments, and thus the crisis stimulates growth. But readjustment requires room to maneuver. Disciplined by fear of unemployment, many adults feel trapped in jobs that no longer meet their needs. Their own inner fears of change are compounded by a narrowing of options. Because it is difficult to find employment, many people cling to jobs that seem dreary and useless.

In a stagnant economy it is harder to move up in the same field. Middle-aged American workers, conditioned to anticipate constant growth in the economy, have lived to see it reach a standstill. Regular promotions and raises can no longer be taken for granted. Pay cuts or token raises aggravate the effects of alienated toil. Increasing numbers of people come home at the end of the day feeling tired, not with the honest fatigue that comes from hard work, but with a draining feeling of having labored without pleasure or pride. Frustrated at work, they contemplate putting their energy elsewhere. But financial realities make it harder to relax from overwork and harder to afford leisure activities. Being poor but happy is a romantic notion of youth. Midlife adults are more likely to be poor and unhappy.

Couples and Money

Financial hardship not only constrains options for the future, but also unravels accommodations worked out in the past. Accommodation is the often painful process of adjustment that takes place when people marry. (Ogden Nash defined marriage as the union of a man who can't sleep with the window closed and a woman who can't sleep with it open.) Once they move in together, two people have to arrange and coordinate the day-to-day routines of life. As single people they were accustomed to making their decisions alone; when they become a couple, each tries to organize the relationship along familiar lines and pressures the other to accommodate. Chief among the many things they have to negotiate is how to handle money. They must decide what money is personal, what will be shared, and who will take care of paying the bills. To the extent that their ideas about money differ, these discussions can be extremely contentious. Many couples are reluctant to discuss money with each other—like sex, it's too full of conflict —but unfortunately, the financial squeeze forces them to re- open this hot topic.

Some couples must also readjust their working patterns, re- defining their relationship in the process. Regardless of what arrangements they would prefer, rising prices and increasing obligations constrain choices. Some married women return to work only to make ends meet; others pass up challenging jobs for the security of jobs they have outgrown. Older and less flexible now, couples are severely strained by the need to renegotiate financial issues. Just when they wanted to think about other things, money once again becomes a daily source of irritation.

Money means power—at work, at home, and in our minds. Men and women on the threshold of middle age are already beginning to question their power. Money woes only add to their anxiety. Men have always measured their self-esteem largely in terms of how much money they earn. Working women are less likely to think of their worth in monetary terms, but contemporary realities make money necessary for survival. Even married women who might prefer a traditional relation- ship, with the husband as major breadwinner, can no longer feel secure without resources of their own.

Divorce doubles the cost of survival. Fear of hardship keeps some bad marriages going, but as long as couples are coerced by economic pressure to stay together, most won't try very hard to make the marriage work. Divorce makes people worse off economically, no matter what the emotional benefits. If eco- nomic straits are severe, psychological benefits are cancelled.

One couple in their late thirties came to me for help after a dozen years of conjoint misery. The "help" they wanted was permission to call it quits. When they finally did so, after an exhaustive but fruitless effort to make things tolerable, it seemed like a good idea. As soon as they were separated each one began to come alive. But gradually the increased financial pressure on both of them eroded their freedom. He moved from the big house that he loved into a small apartment and started working overtime to keep up with child support payments. She did free-lance secretarial work three nights a week, after her regular nine-to-five job. Neither of them had as much time for the children, eating out meant McDonalds, and vacations became a thing of the past. She couldn't even afford to pay a babysitter in order to go out with her friends.

No longer can we assume that everyone gets married before thirty-five. Today many people remain single because, for one reason or another, they question the institution of marriage. Still, many of them move in together, hoping to benefit from the economies of sharing without the trappings of matrimony. Unmarried couples—cohabitors and homosexual partners— are often reluctant to pool their resources. This is a hidden reason for the instability of such relationships. Financial interdependence is a tie that helps hold relationships together in the face of many forces that would pull them apart.

Carmen's success in her job with an automobile corporation helped prove what she was learning in psychotherapy: she was a competent person. Competent performance, however, was the only secure prop she had to an otherwise shaky self-image. She knew she was good at work, but doubted that anyone liked her. When she met Sidney it took a long time for her to believe that anyone so special could possibly love her. She did eventually work through her self-doubt, and the two of them bought a house and moved in together.

Things were fine until Carmen quit her job. Cutbacks, layoffs, and plant closings convinced her that, though she could stay with the company, she would never rise beyond her present position. She took what today is an enormous risk, going back to school to study computer science, while working nights to pay the tuition.

A relationship of equals became unequal. Sidney was willing to pay a larger share of expenses as long as Carmen was in school, but Carmen's uncertainty about her own worth made it hard for her to accept. They had made such a concerted effort to avoid competing or defining their relationship in terms of the amount of money that each one earned. Still, change can unbalance even the best arrangement.

The impact of economic stagnation on the American psyche is also due to inflated expectations. Those reaching middle age in the eighties grew up in an era of unceasing expansion, which led them to become preoccupied with "more" and unable to feel satisfied with less. Growing up after the war, we became avid consumers of advertising, which kept us in a chronic state of unsatisfied desire. Not so unsatisfied as to become disenchanted, though; there was just enough temporary satisfaction to feed our hunger for possessions and keep it alive. As we got older, the due date on the dream kept moving into the future.

Once we reached forty, most of us expected to have it made: a comfortable house, a new car, freedom to travel, perhaps even a vacation home or a boat. Even many of those who were able to afford big ticket luxuries later had to sell them to make ends meet. Ten or twenty years ago it was common for people to reach midlife having achieved a measure of security and satisfaction, and then to reassess their values from material to human. Today's economic conditions make it harder to renounce the sadness of lives centered on accumulation.

Arguments about whether the pinch is due primarily to economic decline or merely to disappointed expectations of "more" are largely irrelevant. People's definition of their situation *is* their reality. The experience of deprivation, which promotes a sense of austerity and a fear of the future, is an indisputable fact of midlife today.

A substantial number of people are hanging on, waiting for things to improve. They don't eat out as often and they repair more things than they replace, but they aren't making any significant changes. The economy may well improve, but this passive strategy is a poor model for tackling the second half of life. Another response is to fight back, working overtime or taking an additional job to keep up, or making creative investments in order to get ahead. The trouble with this approach is that it tends to perpetuate the preoccupation with money.

Changing Sex Roles: Benefits and Pressures

At the same time that they have had to reevaluate their material prospects, today's midlife adults have been confronted with an even more profound change in expectations. Women and men alike have been liberated from the narrow confines of their traditional roles in society. The goal and brightest achievement of the women's movement has been to open doors once closed to women: exterior doors in the workplace and political arena; interior doors of expectation in the hearts of men and women. New possibilities and expectations have created greater freedom, but with it uncertainty and conflict. The variety and complexity of choices puts a great strain on one's sense of self.

Few generations have had to cope with so fundamental a change as a shift in the definition of what it means to be a man or a woman. Once there were distinct social differences that could be depicted without overlap. These differences provided clear-cut roles for men and women: men were strong and dominant, they played rough and made their way to the center of things; women were soft and selfless, so they stayed on the sidelines, serving children—and the men. Psychoanalysts even taught us that these were essential differences, that social roles were a consequence of anatomical distinctions. But anatomy is no longer destiny.

The revival of feminism alerted us to sexual discrimination and pointed the way to more fully realized human roles for all of us. In the process, however, the changes have unloosed many problems. Tension, divorce, family breakdown, and stress-related health concerns have all risen sharply in the wake of the new feminism. The goal of equality is good, but getting there is hard. Children today are growing up in a world not bound by stereotypic conceptions we once took for granted. But men and women born around forty years ago are caught in a social upheaval that greatly complicates their transition to maturity.

Women, ostensibly the primary benefactors of our raised consciousness, inherit the most conflict. Some of these conflicts are manifest and have been frequently described in print. Many women find themselves in a catch-22 situation: mothers are supposed to be at home, but modern women are expected to work outside the home; more and more adults are single or divorced, but people still question whether a woman can be fulfilled outside of marriage. A contemporary woman hears opposing messages at different times from different people. While a woman's mother says one thing, her friends say another. Worse, still, she is likely to get both of these messages from her husband. Since many men are ambivalent about whether or not their wives should work, they are apt to be dissatisfied with whatever her choice is. If she works full-time, her husband will convey his uneasiness about her role change. If she stays at home, even if it is a mutual decision, he may show displeasure with her failure to "do something worthwhile."

There is a widespread belief that men work because they have to and women work because they want to. While both men and women may find personal satisfaction through work-ing, only men's careers are legitimized by the perception of economic necessity. Reality does not match the perception. In *Mothers Who Work,* Jeanne Bodin and Bonnie Mitelman reported the results of an extensive study of the experiences of 442 working mothers. Even though their sample was far from impoverished (the median family income was over forty thou-sand dollars), and the women surveyed felt that working had a positive impact on them emotionally, most started working because they had to. Nevertheless, social institutions are still predicated on the (unwarranted) assumption that a woman's career is optional.

Despite militant protests, women's incomes have remained 60 percent of men's; women are still concentrated in underpaid and overcrowded occupations; and conditions of the workplace are rarely altered to meet the requirements of women who work and take care of children. Those who work while their children are still young usually have to make complicated adjustments to fit work requirements that don't bend. It is hard to develop the kind of flexible work schedule necessary to accommodate small children's needs. Forced to do so, many women seek part-time jobs or accept jobs below their potential. Part-time work is scarce, and quality day care is expensive and often hard to find. Liberals say that day care should be provided directly by business and indirectly through the government in the form of tax incentives. Conservatives point out that putting re-sources into day care means taking them out of other social programs. Meanwhile, working women who are mothers are left to their own devices.

For middle-class women, who generally expect work to be creative and fulfilling, the realities don't often live up to the promise. Women who reenter the workforce after raising chil-dren are likely to find their training inadequate for jobs that match their intellectual capacity. Men, who grew up thinking of work as the essential source of meaning in life, often assume that women, too, must find a career to give purpose to their lives. But work is not a cure for unhappy and frustrated women. Returning to work in midlife may enrich one's life, but the activities that bring us the deepest satisfaction are those related to our earliest ambitions. Work alone will not solve the problems of midlife.

Things are even tougher for working-class women. Work closes in on them earlier and they have fewer options. Most men want their wives to mother them, and while middle-class men *may* make accommodations to their wives who work, working-class men are less likely to do so. Working-class men are especially reluctant to do any "women's work," so their wives work inside and outside the home. Moreover, since the family income is less, the working-class mother is unlikely to have any housecleaning or child-care help. And, unlike her middle-class sister, hers is a job, not a career. As alienated labor, it is a drain on her spirit, rather than a source of enrichment.

Working women with families find the squeeze tight at both ends. Men, raised to expect their wives to take care of the house, are now expected to help. Some do, but not many and not much. In their survey of mothers who work, Bodin and Mitelman found that 95 percent take care of household management, 90 percent take care of meal preparation, 70 percent take care of housecleaning, 93 percent take care of marketing and shopping, and 78 percent take care of the laundry.

Even women who strike a reasonable balance between work and family are constantly pulled in one direction and then the other. As long as they have to juggle the demands of two careers, they cannot put everything into either, though "everything" is often what is demanded of them.

The most serious barrier to occupational equality for women is parenthood. If a child of working parents gets sick, not too many people call the father. This is one reason why less than half of employed women work full-time (U.S. Bureau of the Census, 1980). Working part-time gives many women the flexibility they need, but it creates other problems. Wage rates are lower for part-timers, benefits are reduced or nonexistent, and the occupational choices are few and generally at the low end of the scale. Add to this discrimination against working mothers and the need to work near the home, and you can see the formidable obstacles faced by many women who work.

This, however, still doesn't complete the picture. Changing sex roles have undermined the security of familiar rules for all of us, men and women. Today's forty-year-old woman is caught in a conflict between values she was raised with and roles she is now expected to move into. Women now entering middle age formed their expectations in a very different climate from the one that prevails today. As children growing up in the 1950s, they were not socialized to be competitive or aggressive; as young women in the 1970s, they learned that they were supposed to be. Assertiveness training groups flourished, helping women to overcome institutionalized prejudice, while underscoring that women need to make themselves more powerful. This was especially hard for women raised on fairy tales of princesses who achieve power by marrying a handsome prince.

The strain of transition from traditional to egalitarian gender roles is even harder because it is unexpected. Most of today's middle-aged women did not plan to reenter the labor force, and they did not prepare. They did not finish their training, they did not postpone childbearing—they had a different vision of life after forty. They grew up with a sense of certainty about the future. They dreamed dreams and made plans based on the world as they knew it. Entering maturity, they find that the world has changed. They must change as well.

Men brought up expecting that they would be breadwinners, married to wives who did the housekeeping and took care of the children, are now exposed to a new model. Today's father is encouraged to take on a major share of these duties, to liberate his wife from the drudgery of being one-dimensional and to liberate both of them from being a one-paycheck family. But these men were socialized to put most of their energies into the world of work; when they come home they expect to be taken care of. Now when a forty-year-old husband comes home, his wife may still be at work. When she does come home, they both need a little "mothering." Unfortunately, in many two-paycheck families there isn't enough to go around.

A little strain unites couples; they pitch in and fight as a team. But when the strain is great it becomes divisive. The traditional role division, where men work and women nurture, may have been inequitable, but it did produce stability in the couple and security for the children. When both parents are working, young children must be left to the care of relatives, babysitters, or child-care institutions. Women worry about the quality of that care, while their husbands criticize them for working, or lose respect for themselves for needing the extra income. When working parents come home at the end of the day, they are tired and often under a great deal of stress. What they want most is to relax. But it's hard to relax if you have children eager for your attention. The resulting family interactions are often brief and tense; and the favored activity (television) is passive.

Trouble comes when changes force couples to disrupt their previous balance. As a family therapist, I am frequently asked, what do married couples fight about the most? Not surprisingly money and sex rank near the top. But the greatest number of arguments that I have heard, by far, are about who is going to take out the garbage. The most common case is where a hard-pressed working woman asks her husband to help out a little, and he agrees—perhaps to wash the dishes and empty the garbage. Then, because his heart isn't in it, she has to nag him to do it. One of the saddest aspects of these battles is how embarrassed people are to admit that the mundane matters of life are what really get them down.

Lewis came to the mental health center because of his temper. He described a long history of episodes in which he blew up, started shouting, and often ended by slamming his fist into the wall. Since all of these outbursts occurred during arguments with his wife, I suggested that he bring her to the next session "to help us with the problem."

Lewis and Betty had each been married before. They had one child, a little girl from Betty's previous marriage. As they spoke to each other, I was struck by their total lack of empathy for each other's feelings. When she described how tired she was at night, he countered with his own complaints about working two jobs and coming home to a messy house. She then launched into more grievances—and so on, back and forth in an escalating series of unanswered complaints. Their mutual lack of compassion was sad, but understandable; they were both overwhelmed by endless demands on their time.

Lewis had been attracted to Betty because, unlike his first wife, she listened to him. Marrying her, he thought, would give him a reason to come home at night. Betty saw in Lewis a hard-working, responsible man, and a good father for her daughter. Unhappily, their marriage didn't work out as they planned. The burden of monthly child-care payments from his first marriage forced Lewis to take a second job. Even that wasn't enough, so Betty went to work. Instead of being able to enjoy the prime of life, they were squeezed by financial hardship into such unanticipated and demanding roles that they had nothing left to give each other. No wonder they fought.

How was their problem solved? It wasn't. One of the myths about psychotherapy is that it makes life easier. Life doesn't get any easier, although people may learn how to handle it more effectively. Lewis and Betty's reality was that the dual-career marriage sapped their energy and their patience. The resulting strain eroded their joy in living and their capacity for sympathetic compassion. As a result of therapy, they may have understood this a little better. But it didn't really change things.

Even those of us who are not so hard-pressed have been severely challenged by emotional pressures created by changing sex roles. Men are told that their own lives will be richer and more well-rounded if they take an active part in raising their children. The new ethic is for a man to be softer, gentler, less aggressive, and more nurturant. But this model, like its counterpart—the woman who balances motherhood with a successful career—is easier to preach than to live. True, more women are working and more men are spending a significant amount of time with their children. Nevertheless, the image of a fully integrated career and family life is a mirage. Young people growing up today have time to assimilate the new models and work out more flexible lives. But flexibility comes harder in middle age, and patterns set in youth are difficult to change. The happy consequence of the new vision is that it is an ideal toward which to strive; the unhappy one is that many men now continue to pursue their careers—as they feel they must and as they have been prepared to do since childhood—but now they feel guilty. They feel guilty for their competitive instincts, guilty for not spending more time with their families, guilty for still being traditional men.

One successful lawyer complains that his job takes him away from his children: "I resent those evenings when I have to stay late at the office and can't get home in time to see my son before he goes to bed. I sometimes have to work six or seven days a week, and I'm often upset that it pulls me away from my family." He complains, but it is his choice. Women, caught in the same dilemma, often don't have a choice.

Some people do seem to manage both a successful career and an active role in raising their children. Not too many men do this voluntarily, however. Those who do are usually married to women with careers; some are divorced. Others appear to have freely chosen to balance their own dual roles with their wives'. But these "free choices" are often the result of agitation as much as inspiration. The idea of being involved with their children exerts a strong pull on these men, but so does the pressure of their wives' desires. As with every other aspect of marriage, the choice is not based alone on what individuals think and want; it is worked out in a complicated amalgam of interlocking needs and expectations.

The interlocking balance of a couple's motives is not the only source of unconscious influence on their pattern of career and family lives. Long before they were married, husband and wife were exposed to the example of their parents. Regardless of our conscious attitudes toward our parents' way of life, their model serves as an unconscious template for organizing our own lives. Whether we resolve to emulate or to rebel against them, their behavior shapes our own. One woman, for example, despised her mother's subservience and for that reason did not want to tie herself down to marriage. She chose to live with the man in her life without subjecting herself to "the degrading role of a wife." Nevertheless, during the seven years they lived together, she put "the relationship" ahead of her own self-development. She dropped out of school and took a job with little future in order to help support her partner's career; she neglected her own friends in order to do everything as a couple; and in many other ways she put his needs ahead of her own. While rejecting the trappings of marriage, she settled for her mother's role, but without the protection of a contract. When her partner had a midlife affair, he left. She was devastated. Despite her conscious intention to do otherwise, she had lived out the same traditional pattern as her mother, only without the traditional protection of marriage.

In the 1970s, feminist literature focused on women as victims of a patriarchal culture. What began as a humanistic movement toward liberation became a feminist revolution in which some women gained a feeling of power by personifying men as the enemy. This kind of militancy may be a necessary stage in any social movement that is to attain long-term success. In the short run, however, militancy produces excesses and provokes backlash. My concern is not with moral judgments or sociological predictions, but with the effects of current social conditions on the transition to midlife.

Militant feminism provoked a right-wing, antifeminist backlash. The vocal protests of Phyllis Schlafly galvanized conservative politicians into a visible campaign of opposition, which defeated the Equal Rights Amendment in June of 1982. The rhetorical excesses of the Stop ERA campaign made Schlafly and her cohorts objects of ridicule in liberal, intellectual circles. Yet her dire warnings of the consequences of ERA played on the fears of new roles in ordinary men and women, who killed the Equal Rights Amendment with their silent lack of support.

Another reaction to the women's movement involved men's liberation. At first, sensitive men learned to guard their impulses and attitudes, lest they be condemned as "male chauvinists." Later, they learned to take advantage of the new freedom. Men began to shed the façade of a masculinity fastidiously devoid of tenderness. They donned softer and brighter clothes, wore their hair longer, and allowed themselves to show their feelings with candor and naturalness once associated with "femininity." The men's movement was part accommodation to women's demands for change and part rebellion against the traditional male breadwinner role. According to Barbara Ehrenreich in *The Hearts of Men*, the current male rebellion made its first rumblings in the 1950s, in the form of the gray flannel attack on "conformity." Middle- and upper-middle-class men began to resent the sterile routines they followed in order to support their families in the suburbs. Later, the movement had its first manifesto in the unlikely guise of *Playboy* magazine, which told men that they were better off single. If a man wanted a woman, he could rent one for the price of drinks and dinner. Teenage boys eagerly gaped at the large-breasted models on the centerfold. So did middle-aged men, but they also read Hugh Hefner's editorial attacks on marriage and self-sacrifice. Sexual titillation may have been the come-on, but the real message was escapist—from duty, from responsibility, and especially, from the "breadwinner ethic."

The human potential movement of the sixties offered a different way out for men who felt themselves trapped by family obligations. In place of repression and performance, humanistic psychology offered "self-actualization." In theory, this meant expressing one's full potential for living—men could be sensitive and women could be assertive. In practice, it often translated into solipsistic emotionalism, and many people sought emotional satisfaction away from their families, in encounter groups and artificial communities that grew up around the new therapies. Self-improvement became self-absorption. Restless men began to think of their obligations to others as onerous and repressive, and longed to shuck them off. The excuse they needed was to come from an unlikely source.

In the seventies, the women's movement set out to liberate women from financial and emotional dependency. In the process, men became freer than ever before to abandon the bread-winning role. Divorce is now easier and more acceptable. When a marriage breaks up, the man becomes single, with a whole new industry catering to his needs. Meanwhile, his wife is likely to become a single mother.

By choice or circumstance, many women are now faced with the logistics of being single at a time when they expected to be mated for life. For women living on their own, life is often harder, complicated by the scarcity of free heterosexual men and frequently by the strain of raising children alone. The practical burden on single-parent families is doubled. Most of the time, this burden falls on the woman. Single mothers have less help and less company. Working, housecleaning, shopping, cooking, carpooling, and washing clothes eats up the single parent's time and energy. The relatively few fathers with sole custody quickly discover that, despite what was portrayed in *Kramer vs. Kramer,* the job is a lot harder than learning to make French toast.

An increasing number of men and women are unattached in midlife. It isn't always a conscious choice. Sometimes they can't find the "right" partner. They go to health clubs, attend countless parties, take out personal ads, vacation at Club Med, and frequent bars that cater to singles. Commercial packaging makes these activities seem glamorous—especially to discontented married people—but the reality of the dating scene is not so glamorous. Movies like *Looking for Mr. Goodbar* and *Single Bars, Single Women* have dramatized the loneliness of the bar scene. Most of the women portrayed in these movies are in their twenties, and this may be the majority. But go to any singles bar and you will also find women a little older—it doesn't get any easier for them.

Men, often portrayed as insensitive predators in films on the single life, have their own troubles. But a scarcity of available women is not one of them. By forty, single women outnumber men by more than two to one. In another generation, most of them would have been married. But now, with more acceptable choices, many people are particular. They want freedom and self-expression and are often afraid of the compromise and self-sacrifice that marriage requires. The specter of total commitment—a lifetime of responsibilities and children—keeps them from settling down. Many who pass thirty-five still single feel desperate about their chances *and* inadequate about themselves. Many, however, were tied up during the prime marriage years. One woman was too busy with medical studies to date; another had a five-year relationship that almost, but not quite, ended in marriage. She discovered that when you get older it's harder to bounce back from rejection.

Sociologist Jessie Bernard once argued that men need marriage more than women, because men are dependent on women to take care of them. Perhaps, but the majority of women entering midlife in the 1980s are economically dependent and highly vulnerable. As long as divorce laws are loose and the economy is tight, women who planned their lives as part of a family unit will be permanently insecure. So far, the main benefactors of women's liberation are men.

The cumulative impact of these changes undermined the sense of obligation that supports the nuclear family and taught men to question traditional concepts of masculinity. Among educated professionals, "macho" became a term of derision, and "authenticity" became the great virtue. Men are now free to drop the John Wayne persona and be who they want. These men are now allies in women's struggle against stereotypes. As militant attacks on men began to subside, "sexist" replaced "male chauvinist" as the favored label of opprobrium. The attack on prejudicial stereotypes brought all forms of gender roles into question. Difference itself was suspect, because it was thought to doom women to second-class status. Sexual androgyny became the new ideal.

The androgyny of feminist theory was actually practiced by the flower children of the 1960s. But the flower children were concerned more with sex than sexism. Their protest was against violence and middle-class consumerism. They were interested in "peace and love," not masculine and feminine stereotypes. Their androgynous style was more a uniform than a program. Still, they introduced "unisex" fashions into the mainstream culture and provided an example of androgyny that seemed attractive to their elders.

The evil of sexism is economic and social exploitation of women by men. It is perpetuated by false stereotypes, according to which men and women are inverse images of each other. Any trait appropriate to one gender is inappropriate to the other. Thus if men are strong, women are weak; if women are sensitive, men are thick-skinned. Obviously, both sexes lose when their roles are polarized this way. Just as obviously, the solution should be to do away with the false stereotypes. The trouble is that it is very hard to bring about negative change. It's harder to *stop* doing something than to *start* doing something. For example, most people prefer to "be on a diet" than to "eat less." Smokers usually substitute some other activity, such as eating Lifesavers, when they try to quit. The need to substitute something active and positive is especially strong when a person tries to change something that he or she is addicted to.

Older people are not particularly worried about being called sexist. They either ignore the label or don't care. Today's children also have a different experience; nobody told them that little girls can't play soccer, or that little boys can't learn to cook. It's the group in the middle who are so concerned about eradicating sexism—breaking down barriers and stamping out vestiges of prejudice in themselves.

Freedom from stereotypes is one thing, androgyny is another. To be androgynous—actually, to aspire to be androgynous—means to deny parts of the self. For some women, it means to seek physical power and dominance in imitation of men, not to release their own potential. Acting out an androgynous role is no better than acting out the role of he-man or ultrafeminine woman.

Leading writers on sex roles are now developing a countertheme, namely that men and women are different. Several writers with impeccable credentials in the women's movement, including Carol Gilligan, Maggie Scarf, Jean Baker Miller, and Betty Friedan, have described women as more relationship-oriented and men as more achievement-oriented. The danger of this trend is that of returning to separate but unequal status; the advantage is of helping people, men and women, recognize their own unique potentials. If women are different, the differences are as likely to be strengths as they are weaknesses.

There are, of course, logical reasons why women should be different from men. Women alone have the biological equipment for bearing and suckling babies. Brought up with a caretaker of the same sex, little girls have a formative influence toward being more empathic than independent. Ten or twenty years from now these differences will probably have been spelled out and generally agreed upon. But that will be too late to guide today's middle-aged adults, who are caught in the ambiguities of transition.

The Computer Revolution

The third great cultural transformation of the 1980s is the computer revolution. Since its introduction in 1949, the electronic computer has proliferated at an explosive rate, revolutionizing our culture in the process. By 1977, a half million of these machines had been installed in the United States, according to the International Data Corporation. By contrast, nearly eight million personal computers were sold in 1984 alone. Before the end of this decade, twenty million Americans will be working with computers. People are using them in homes, offices, factories, schools, and places of entertainment. Computers are used for storing and analyzing data, word processing, and playing electronic games; they can regulate traffic, replace filing clerks, and play chess.

Still, we are told, grand masters can beat even the most sophisticated computer at chess. Creative souls have special gifts of intuition that no machine can duplicate. Moreover, as scholars are fond of pointing out, there is no such thing as a logic of discovery, and therefore no way to computerize inventiveness. Why do some people take such delight in emphasizing the computer's limits? Because we are scared. No one takes the time to bring an inconsequential threat down to size.

The machines are scary. Even the arcade games can be intimidating. Their flashing lights, electronic bleating, and futuristic themes make them seem like something from outer space. Kids love it. Anything that looks like *Star Wars* suits them just fine. The result is a disorienting parent-child role reversal.

Our kids are growing up with the computer. They are introduced to it at an early age, not just in the arcades, but in school as well. Children are almost equally as enthralled by doing math on the school computer as they are by playing Space Invaders in the neighborhood arcade. Theirs is the future, and it will undoubtedly be enriched by computer technology.

Everywhere it is introduced the computer brings the advantages of fast and efficient problem-solving and communication. But the advantages are mostly for the young and the few who understand the technology. For midlife adults, computers only increase feelings of obsolescence and isolation.

The vast majority of adults in midlife find the computer intimidating. The marketing industry knows this. That's why they promulgated the slogan "user friendly," one of the most vacuous and manipulative phrases ever invented. That it persists demonstrates that it strikes home.

Kids think of their parents as "out of it" because they are not involved with the latest enthusiasms. Every era has new technology and every generation may feel the world is passing them by. Technological fads, of course, come and go. Some go the way of the Edsel. But the computer, like the telephone and television, looks like a permanent fixture. We have to learn to use computers; many forty-year-olds feel too old to learn—and too young to admit it. A case in point is the chemistry professor who told me, "I don't really need a computer in my work, but I finally bought one so that I could at least speak the language." Bits and bytes, RAMS and ROMS, and floppy disks—hearing these terms tossed around underscores the feeling of ignorance in the uninitiated.

Even those bewildered parents who successfully avoid computers at work may eventually succumb to pressure to buy one as a learning device for their children. (Middle-class parents seem ever willing to mortgage their lives for their children's future.) "Come on, Fred, if we don't buy one for the kids they'll lose out at school." When the parents finally do succumb they are likely to find themselves left behind. To kids, computers are a fact of life, not some newfangled form of technology. After all, how many kids have trouble relating to anything that looks like a TV set? Middle-aged adults may be intimidated by machines, but most kids have a machine—the TV—for a best friend. The home computer may even take over from the TV, serving a function similar to that once served by kittens and puppies; the computer never gets mad, and it's always there.

Home computers are used to play games, prepare tax returns, moniter investments, write résumés, and even pay bills. Microcomputers also enable people to work at home. Some of these home users are professionals; some are part-time clerical workers. Remote office work has the obvious advantage of flexibility, especially valuable for the parents of small children. But homeworking also carries the risk of exploitation and increased isolation. Working outside the office means working away from the benevolent protection of unions and government regulators. Piece-rate work at home was made illegal in order to eliminate ghetto sweatshops. The computerese euphemism for piece rate is "work unit," but it means the same thing and it has the same risks.

A computerized society is likely to be an alienated society. Office workers, tethered to computer consoles, will be separated from each other. Families will disperse to personal computers much as they now cluster around the communal television. These changes are still in the future, but we are already feeling the alienating effects of the computer.

Computerization has taken the human element out of many service transactions, leaving us feeling cut off and powerless. Many of our bills now come with strange-looking electronic lettering, and if there is an error we have a devil of a time trying to straighten it out. Nobody seems to be responsible.

Expensive technology, of which the computer is only the most visible symbol, enhances the impersonal bureaucratic power of private and government institutions. Centralized power is more efficient, but it limits freedom and robs the citizenry of privacy. Computerization has made possible widespread gathering of information from one source—possibly friendly—to another—possibly unfriendly. You don't have to be a secret agent or a criminal to be on file somewhere; we all are.

Regardless of how they feel about the new technology, middle-aged adults are having to cope with its impact on the factory, the office, and the home. Most people's first and most immediate concern is with a loss of jobs. There will be some new jobs in industries that manufacture electronics and in research and development. Once again, though, these jobs go primarily to the young and to a small corps of experts. Workers over thirty are liable to find themselves replaced or their jobs downgraded. Age sets an early limit on which workers industrial managers are willing to retrain.

Already some factory workers are being replaced by industrial robots—in what sociologist Daniel Bell calls "The Third Industrial Revolution." These machines bear little resemblance to the humanlike gadgets of Capek's play *RUR*, which contributed the word "robot" to our language, or to the endearing "androids" in *Star Wars*. They are actually computer-controlled, jointed arms, which can hold a variety of tools, such as drills, wrenches, and spray-paint guns. These "steel-collar workers" do jobs that are dull, dangerous, and dirty. They are now confined mainly to the assembly lines of automobile factories. Eventually, though, the net loss of jobs from computerization will be considerable.

Equally important is the impact of computerization on the nature of jobs and the working atmosphere. The most optimistic outlook is for a reduction of drudgery and the elimination of dirty jobs. Remember, though, the driving motivation of American industry is to increase productivity and short-term profit. The long-range results of this thinking can be seen in the deterioration of American railroads, where tracks are repaired when new roadbeds are needed, and the decay of American factories, where an inadequate share of the profits has been reinvested in plant equipment. Not too many workers will benefit from computerization.

So far the computer's most dramatic impact has been on office work. Mountains of paper are now reduced to tiny electronic chips, and calculations that once took hours can now be done with great speed and little effort. Service industries, like banking and insurance, are in the vanguard, because their collection, analysis, and dissemination of information are tasks uniquely suited to the computer's capabilities. We now do much of our banking with computerized machines, many given folksy nicknames ("Tillie the Teller") in an attempt to mask the dehumanized nature of the transaction. The fully automated office may still be in the future, but that future is not far off for branch banking.

The mystique of the computer, with its aura of scientific benevolence, is such that it seems entirely positive. Most people are familiar with its virtues and expect it to be a boon to office workers. It turns out, however, that the people singing the praises of office automation frequently happen to be computer salesmen.

On the dark side of office automation are displacement and isolation—anxious fears of midlife. Investing in expensive machines is economically feasible only if it results in a reduction of the workforce. (The alternative, increased production, occurs in some companies, but is no longer possible on a large scale.) Since it is not clear where large numbers of redundant office workers will find employment, anxiety is high, especially among older and less-skilled employees.

Computerization creates a well-defined class system in many large offices. While there are some new, highly technical jobs, there is a more rapid expansion of lower level jobs. Technology dichotomizes the workforce into the few who understand the nature of the mechanical operations and the many who merely push the buttons. American secretaries have long been a technological underclass. Computerization seems certain to accelerate this trend. Once the novelty of using the word processor wears off, secretaries become drones, deprived of the more complex and interesting tasks that once broke up the tedium of typing.

The shift from paper to electronics in office work allows routine tasks to be performed quickly. But the result for most workers is more volume rather than more variety. At the same time the pace of their work is speeded up, these workers are isolated from co-workers and more intensely supervised. A terminal on every desk means controlled and monitored work, increased stress, and reduced human contact. An employee tied down to a computer terminal is isolated, not only from other office workers, but also from a sense of the overall process of the office. When this happens the employee is likely to feel like an insignificant cog in a large piece of machinery. Along with drudgery comes a sense of meaninglessness.

Am I painting an unrealistically bleak picture of computerized offices? What about all the exciting new jobs? The Bureau of Labor Statistics estimates that approximately 685,000 new jobs will be created in the computer industry in the 1980s. These include computer operators, computer technicians, computer programmers, systems analysis, and other computer specialists. The more creative of these jobs require extensive training and thus will go primarily to the young and, incidentally, to men. Middle-aged workers, especially women, will continue to be concentrated at the low end of the spectrum. Seventy-eight percent of the women in computer occupations work either as keypunchers or computer operators, while only 31 percent of men in computer jobs are in these positions. Most of the opportunities in the computer field are in the future.

Computers are not insidious engines of evil, and they will not corrupt or destroy us any more than the machines of the first industrial revolution did. In the long run the advantages of computerization may outweigh the disadvantages. But getting there will take time, and the average person now entering middle age will not reap the benefits.

Each of the social changes discussed in this chapter exerts a special strain on adults in midlife. The stagnant economy constrains our options and prolongs our preoccupation with material success. Changing sex roles offer new options, but also pressure and conflict. Computer technology opens new horizons, but its promise seems brighter to youngsters and specialists. Together these trends have a cumulative effect on us all. But they seem to affect some more than others.

Some people succumb to adversity, others thrive on it. But the fact that there can be so much variation in our responses seems to indicate that events themselves don't determine our final response. In later chapters, we'll explore what there is inside us that causes us to react to the pressures of midlife in so many different ways.

4

The Pain of Crisis

THE expression "If it isn't broken, don't fix it" can be applied to things human as well as mechanical. By the time we are settled into adulthood, it usually takes a strong disruption to induce change. A midlife crisis is—or can be—a disquieting inspiration, as inner rumblings provoke a variety of reactions. These reactions may be constructive or destructive. But all have one common denominator. No matter what course of action people choose, the majority act to dispel the unhappy feelings, not to change the conditions that produced them in the first place. Most of the destructive reactions to midlife share a single purpose: they are designed to mask the emotions that signal the need to change.

Insidious depression, negativism, withdrawal, chronic anxiety, and self-preoccupation are symptoms that something is wrong. If we recognize a crisis, we can try to cope. We can turn to familiar remedies that have worked in the past—calling for help, keeping busy, getting in shape, or tackling new projects. Or we can channel our energies into constructive and satisfying outlets—new careers, new relationships, or renewed enthusiasm for old ones. Unfortunately, many people act before the feelings that propel them reach the level of consciousness.

In childhood, when we were pursued by demons, we panicked and ran away. Later, much later, we learned that not all those demons were real. The demon of midlife is time itself, or so it seems. Many of the destructive pursuits of these years are frenzied attempts to reverse, or at least halt, the passage of time.

We know it isn't grown-up to run away when things don't work out, but as most grown-ups know, you don't have to move your feet to run away. When we first stumble on the major issues of midlife, many of us feel helpless. Operating according to invisible, unexamined rules, we seem unable to break out of all that constricts us. Sometimes the pain is too much, and we push it away or blame the nearest scapegoat. Spouses, bosses, children, responsibility, and the government all seem to conspire against our happiness and fulfillment. At a time when we might be developing more concern for others, we turn inward instead, seeking personal gratification or becoming bitter if we can't seem to find it.

It does no good to pass judgment on such negative responses to crisis. Understanding that our reactions function to distract us from the hard task of self-examination is the first step toward doing something about them. When the subjective discomfort is too much, it's only human to gravitate to anything that can insulate us.

Alcohol, Drugs, and Avoidance

Many people retreat into excessive drinking, drug abuse, self-pity and depression, or psychosomatic ailments. In the 1980s there has been an enormous increase in the incidence of anorexia, bulimia, and just plain overeating. Also on the rise are panic disorders and agoraphobia—disorders that primarily affect women. The proliferation of these maladies testifies to the magnitude of stress in contemporary American life. Sometimes these reactions are transient and reversible. When they reach major proportions, it is no longer useful to speak of a midlife crisis. Any of the serious forms of substance abuse or emotional disorder can be touched off by the conflicts of the midlife transition, but when that does happen we need to consider the unique properties of the disorder—alcoholism, depression, or whatever—and turn to the proven techniques for dealing with such problems. Someone who drinks a fifth of whiskey a day needs an alcohol treatment program, not a book on the midlife crisis.

More common than these dramatic disorders are insidious versions of withdrawal, which, because they stay closer to normal limits, may escape notice. No one but the person involved may notice the anxious dependence on two or three drinks at the end of the day, substituting the television set for real human contact, or the constant feeling that life isn't worth living.

People in conflict over their impulses and urges may use alcohol to dissolve their inhibitions (the conscience is soluble in alcohol). Later, when guilty self-recrimination sets in, they may console themselves by drinking again. The sedative properties of alcohol are well-known, and the number of people who regularly find relief from stress and depression is large. Drinking, in moderation, is not necessarily destructive, but two aspects make it detrimental. Drinking often fogs the sense that something is wrong and needs to be changed. And drinking can become a compulsion.

The addictive potential of alcohol or drugs is increased when we discover that they provide predictable relief from anxiety. Moreover, the number of people who recognize their dependence on drink is a small fraction of the total. A surprising number of people would find it difficult to prove that they aren't dependent on alcohol (or some other drug) by giving it up for seven days—one short week.

For many people, drinking activates a sense of well-being not found elsewhere in their experience. Unlike getting high on accomplishment or love, alcohol has the advantage of being easy to control—that is, in the sense that the drinker can choose when and where to uncork the good feelings from the bottle. A lot of men choose to drink in the company of other men, where alcohol not only deadens the pain, but also gives them the courage to find solace in company. Later, the old saying "First the man takes a drink, then the drink takes the man" can become an ugly reality. Women also drink socially, of course, but more of them drink at home. Solitary drinking has for years been a silent affliction of stay-at-home wives. The shame of drinking—of needing to drink—deprives them of even the chance to share their misery.

Drugs are and have been more widely used by people younger than midlife. The majority of those turning forty in the eighties have experimented with marijuana, but may no longer smoke anything. Some have tried the new glamour drug, cocaine, but most of us shy away from it. A forty-year-old with a drug problem is more likely trying to get by than to get high. Many of us depend on something to make us sleep, keep our blood pressure down, improve our digestion, or narcotize our anxieties. Our chemical crutches are more likely to come from the drugstore than the street.

Instead of deadening ourselves to all feeling, some of us seek escape by grasping for more. But rather than searching for satisfaction in the main business of our lives, we smuggle gratification outside the confines of family and career. And in the process we may risk destroying our families.

Extramarital Affairs

Sexual infidelity is the most notorious product of a midlife crisis, perhaps because it is so common and has so many painful repercussions. We see adultery portrayed so often in books and movies that it has become a cliché. When Tom Ewell schemes to get Marilyn Monroe to scratch his "Seven-Year Itch," amused audiences see it as a harmless game.

By today's standards, *The Seven-Year Itch* seems tame, even quaint. Infidelity is a favorite theme of television and movie producers, and on HBO we can now see in graphic detail what was once only hinted at. All this exposure numbs our shock to the idea of sex outside of marriage. Extramarital sex on the screen may lead to problems for the characters, but our distance from them makes us likely to underestimate the potential consequences of infidelity.

No one knows precisely how common extramarital sex is—participants don't register with the census bureau—but estimates put the figure fairly high. Interview data on incidence originated with the Kinsey report in 1953. This evidence, together with subsequent studies, suggests that approximately 50 percent of married men have had affairs, while 30 percent of married women have been unfaithful. Sex outside the relationship is even more common in homosexual couples (more so among gay men than lesbian women) and in heterosexual couples who are living together but not married.

Infidelity is now more frequently discussed than ever. Nevertheless, the incidence does not seem to have changed in recent years. Men and women today are more likely to have premarital sex than in the past, and the fact that more married women are now working means that there are more opportunities for extramarital sex in midlife. Extramarital sex is not confined to midlife, of course; people succumb to temptation at twenty-five as well as thirty-five, at fifty as well as forty. But, according to many studies, the number of extramarital affairs reaches a peak at age forty.

Those who are involved may not question why they are attracted to extramarital relationships; to them it seems obvious. But the motivation, for both men and women, to seek sex outside of marriage is not always what it seems.

Boredom is an often cited cause of extramarital sex. While young couples may feel that their sexual relationship is sacred, years with the same partner can make it seem profane. "My marriage was *so boring,*" a man or a woman may say; "I was looking for something—anything—to put a little excitement back into my life." The boredom may have little to do with sex, but many people turn to sex, like alcohol, as a quick fix.

Boredom may be the prevailing experience that drives some people into extramarital sex, but it is not the cause. Boredom is a derivative emotion that masks conflict and projects blame outward. When we are bored it is usually in self-defense; something we don't want to face is making us anxious. Because midlife arouses many anxieties, we may throw up a protective smoke screen. Instead of reorganizing the way we are living, we do what we always wanted to do: we break the monotony with novelty. And what could be a more exciting place to find novelty than in the bedroom!

At midlife many couples couple more out of habit than desire. Some people try to animate their sex lives with romance and novelty—or wish their spouse would. Women are often expected singlehandedly to spice up married life. Magazines like *Cosmopolitan* promote sexual allure as a means for single women to get power and married women to keep it. Country songs (written from a man's point of view) admonish women to discourage their men from straying by keeping them happy in the bedroom. But there are limits to how exciting the same partner can be after fifteen or twenty years. That helps explain the fascinating effect of sex with a stranger. These liaisons have none of the predictability of habit, and sex with a new partner helps us forget that we are growing older.

Infidelity and Self-Image

One of the persistent forces behind extramarital affairs is the need to shore up a faltering self-image. When midlife is a time of disappointments, nothing soothes the spirit more than love from someone who makes you feel special. Often that someone turns out to be someone new.

In marriage, we are revealed without glamour. If your spouse no longer thinks of you as a scintillating and romantic figure, it may not be—as many people fear—because he or she knows the real you. Rather, people lose appeal for their spouses over the years because they no longer put much effort into the relationship. Marriage is a closed relationship in which it is difficult to get a reliable sense of self-worth. We come to take each other for granted: "Does she (or he)," we wonder, "stay with me because she (or he) loves me, or only because we are married?" For that reason, many of us in midlife—when we are already questioning our own value—become even more sensitive to the opinions of others.

Like it or not, physical attractiveness is a major determinant of feelings of self worth. None of us is immune to vanity. At a certain age both men and women begin to wonder about their ability to attract the opposite sex. Little flirtations are playful attempts to console ourselves with proof that we are still attractive. If the response is good, we feel a renewed sense of confidence, sometimes charged with sexual undertones.

Some people don't stop with consoling flirtations. Either by design or by impulse, the flirtation escalates into an affair. When barriers of conscience are low or the need for reassurance is high, some people take lovers, using sex defensively to prove their adequacy and desirability. They need their lovers' caresses to stroke their egos.

So what's so bad about that?

The mythology of romance (love conquers all) leads many people to overestimate their ability to control or contain an affair. Keeping it secret seems to work for some people, yet many of these feel they can never again be truly open and honest with their spouses. Revelation is equally unpredictable. Trust in a marriage is implicitly founded on monogamy, and therefore adultery threatens the stability of marriage and the family.

Sexual passions can be ignited in many ways; even after years of predictable fidelity, the unpredictable can happen before anyone has time to think. Take the case of Roger, a reasonably happy (or so he thought) husband. Although he enjoyed looking at other women, he never seriously considered having an affair and would have said it was out of the question.

Then came the business trip to Cleveland. Roger rarely traveled, and when he did, he didn't like it much. When business meetings were over, he usually just hung around his hotel room watching television. This time, however, he ran into Lori Jean, an old acquaintance he hadn't seen in years. Although he was usually shy and didn't make friends easily, Roger somehow felt the need to open up. They had several drinks and talked for hours. Since Lori Jean was staying in the same hotel, it seemed only friendly to walk her to her door. The good-night kiss that started as a friendly gesture soon turned into a passionate embrace, and then they were inside the room. Roger was beyond thinking; before he realized it, he had broken a standard he wholeheartedly believed in.

Afterward, remorse set in. At first it was the morbid fear "What if I get herpes?" He didn't think it likely, but he went to his doctor for reassurance. Once that anxiety was dispelled, Roger felt the full force of his guilt and worry. He felt guilty for what he had done, but even more worried that his wife would find out. From Roger's point of view, his mistake was having done something forbidden and inherently wicked; from mine, as his therapist, it was that he hadn't thought about the consequences of his behavior and wasn't prepared to accept them.

Roger's behavior is easy to condemn, especially for those who have never faced a similar situation. Those who have not may envy him (not knowing the anguish he was in for) or fail to understand (not knowing the power of impulses that get out of control).

What happens next varies widely. The simplest solution is the least likely and the most risky. Roger could simply confess to his wife and ask her forgiveness (thereby dumping the burden of his guilt on her). But this rarely happens. Despite all the talk of more liberal sexual mores, extramarital sex generally remains secretive. Roger won't tell her. He is afraid she will fall apart or never forgive him. His conspiratorial silence now leaves the door open to other possibilities. Perhaps he will see the other woman again, and perhaps they will become infatuated, even hopelessly entangled. Not having been found out, Roger may repeat the experience with another woman. As long as he blames his frustration on his wife, he may feel free to "cheat" again once his fear of discovery fades. Or maybe Roger will simply live with his secret and privately renew his vow of fidelity.

Roger's experience—actually, Roger's and Lori Jean's; we only looked at his side of it—is typical of many stories I have heard from men. Away from home, an unexpected (and unprepared for) opportunity presents itself, and they are swept away. We might call this the "Eve Tempted Me" syndrome.

Men rely on years of practiced compartmentalization and women's traditional inaccessibility to separate fantasies from deeds. Given the chance—for example, when the approach is made by a woman—they are not accustomed to saying no. By rationalizing that they are powerless against impulses aroused by the other person, they let themselves off the hook. It isn't them, it is "temptation." Another, equally common group of men are angry and deliberate; projecting the blame for their dissatisfaction onto the women in their lives makes them feel entitled to retaliation.

It may still be a man's world politically and economically, but many men feel powerless in their own homes. Successful men travel around in a world where they are catered to. They fly first class at the expense of their companies, eat in elegant restaurants, and delegate tedious tasks to subordinates. Nurses and secretaries make them feel special, entitled. When they come home, they see a more provincial environment. The once-exciting women they married have become lackluster in the role of homemaker, and—what intimidates men most—they are mothers. The natural bond between mothers and children is solidified in the thirties when most men are too preoccupied at the office to squeeze their way into these firmly fixed coalitions. A lot of men assert their domination in pornographic fantasies, with no real expectations of translating them into action. Yet the possibility is there. Many men are away from home a good deal, and there they come in contact with younger women, some of whom no longer require men to make the first move. Furthermore, because of their career status, many of these women are vulnerable to sexual exploitation. When men do take advantage of illicit opportunities, their actions are often initiated or sustained by hostility.

In extramarital affairs, what appears to be a purely sexual drive is equally likely to be a form of aggressive acting out. Many men at midlife feel tired from hard work and frustrated by years of stifled desire. Some believe passionately that their wives are frigid. Perhaps this explanation is less unsettling than thinking of themselves as conflicted or inadequate. If they see their wives as resistant and frustrating barriers to enjoyment, they can turn to other women. But when they reduce these women to objects of sexual pleasure, their frustration is not likely to subside. The deeper gratification and enjoyment they yearn for still eludes them.

The much-publicized sexual liberation of younger people can also make middle-aged men feel left out. Many fathers are competitive and envious of their own adolescent children. The vast opportunities open to adolescents stir up dormant impulses, making parents scared, jealous, and angry. They also assume that their friends have it better than they do—few men actually share confidences about their sex lives, except perhaps to brag about (real or imagined) conquests. Looking around they see sex everywhere. Highly romanticized public displays titiliate and preoccupy them with false expectations. They begin to see marriage as a trap and react passively, blaming their wives and bemoaning the fact that they were born into the "wrong" generation.

Women are angry too, though their anger often dwells beneath the surface. Until quite recently women were expected to suppress their sexual needs in order to please the men in their lives. Despite the cultural mythology of uncontrollable male sexuality, it is of course women who can have multiple orgasms and are physically capable of having sex countless times without tiring. Today, women are more likely to assert their own rights to satisfaction. In the process, some turn angrily away from marriage to seek satisfaction in outside relationships. Certain radical feminists go so far as to argue that a woman who commits herself to one man is collaborating in her own oppression and that traditional marriage is akin to slavery. These angry voices probably do not speak for the average woman, but they do capture some of her frustration.

Most women are angry, not at the institution of marriage, but at the particular man they married. Many of them feel deprived, unfulfilled, and cheated. In this respect they are no different from their male counterparts, but, unlike men, women are more likely to be interested in a rewarding relationship than in casual sex. The relationship is likely to come first, and for this reason there is greater likelihood that infidelity will develop into a sustained extramarital affair. With men sex sometimes leads to romance, sometimes not. Women usually tell a different story; romance comes first, then maybe sex.

When Ann Landers wrote a column about a man who was contemplating a penile implant because he was impotent, she was flooded with mail from women who said nuts to the implant. Sexual intercourse was not what they really wanted. What they valued most was hugging, holding close, and words of tenderness (presumably missing from their lives). Landers said she was astonished at the number of letters and the similarity of response.

Women often begin extramarital relationships without sex; some even keep it that way. In these affairs without sex, the participants may think of themselves as "just friends." The friends may be colleagues who frequently meet for lunch, or they may be members of a common interest group who go out of their way to be alone together. They may not recognize the potential of their prolonged nonsexual relationship to become an extramarital affair as long as their desires remain unconscious or are resisted.

An undercurrent of sexual vibration between friends adds an extra measure of pleasure to the relationship. Mature men and women can enjoy this mutual appreciation without undue anxiety if they know how to feel without acting. Sexual attraction between friends becomes a problem if the eroticized relationship prevents them from confronting deficiencies in their primary relationships. Even if they never go to bed together, many of these people are escaping from unsatisfactory marriages. If they are surreptitious about their meetings, this is a clue that they have something to hide.

Eventually, however, standards of personal morality may falter in the face of instinctual desires, teased out of hiding by prolonged intimacy. When sex does become a part of the relationship, it is usually much better than it was in the marriage. "Illicit" sex is not dulled by habit or burdened by all the conflicts of the marriage bed.

Consider Ellen's experience, a story that I have heard from at least half a dozen other women. She was having an affair; she was in love. What she didn't understand was why or how it happened. As far as she could tell, there was nothing wrong with her life. Her husband, Jerry, was the right kind of man—

industrious, successful—and things were pretty much what she was brought up to expect. A house in the suburbs, two little girls, and now a satisfying job as a personnel officer—weren't these the ingredients of "the good life"?

Ellen met Mark at work. He was an ex-priest and, like her, keenly interested in human relationships. In the beginning they were just friends. But when she talked he listened; it was not the dutiful half-attentive listening that Jerry offered, but a palpable absorption in what she had to say. With Mark she felt alive, all over.

Ellen knew she was infatuated with Mark before she knew what to do about it. She fantasized about a short period of intense romance that would leave her marriage untouched. Her values told her this was wrong, but she couldn't stop thinking about going to bed with him. Before she thought it through, he made the first move and she forgot her reservations.

Afterward, she wasn't sure what to think or what to do; she just needed to get out of there, so she went right home. She took the afternoon off and spent it vacuuming, dusting, and cleaning up—in a frenzied attempt to put her house in order. Even though she was a successful professional woman, in a crisis she fell back on the role she learned would make her a "good girl." Later, when she had time to reflect, she realized that something had gone out of her marriage, but she decided to keep what she had rather than take a chance on what might be. She kept her secret and tried to revive her marriage.

While men are likely to have a conscious sexual motive for infidelity, married women are usually drawn to an emotional involvement that is missing from their marriages. This difference is a product of early training, reinforced by the conditions of adult life. Teenage boys are taught that it's okay to fool around—limits are set by the girls; marriage, not sex, is the serious business. According to leading women writers Carol Gilligan and Jean Baker Miller, women's lives are organized by attachment and affiliation; men, however, seem to retain their capacity for detachment.

Men seem better able than women to compartmentalize their relationships. At first, the other woman seems to be the lover a man has been waiting for all his life. She's beautiful, sensitive, highly sexed—*and* she adores him. In truth, some people are only able to express certain feelings outside the family, with all its commitment and responsibility. Marital sex may be dulled by familiarity and complicated by bad memories; if we go deeper, we discover conflicts—a fear of dependency, for example—that make it hard for many people to be sexually free with a married partner.

Most people are generous with blame for their dissatisfaction; if marriage is a drag, it's the spouse's fault. The same dynamic applies to women as well as men, but women who are dissatisfied are likely to shed one mate and choose another; men are more willing to split themselves between relationships. The chief concern of men who cheat is of getting caught; married women are more likely to be frustrated by not being able to see their lovers when they want to. Men with two part-time partners cope with conflicting feelings by permitting only feelings of duty and obligation for their wives, while expressing the instinctual side of their natures with extramarital partners.

The Aftermath of Infidelity

Not all infidelity is destructive. And the effects vary so much that it is hazardous to generalize—or easy to bend the facts to fit whatever your point of view happens to be. Extramarital sex can be an isolated event, or even series of events, that leaves the marriage untouched, at least in obvious ways. It can even be a positive experience—a crisis within a crisis that leads to renewal. Entwined with apparently destructive instinctual manifestations are hidden potentials for growth and development. Sexual impulses contain the seeds of a more zestful life and deeper interpersonal relationships.

Some people change partners with good results. Others are reawakened by an affair to the possibility of a more passionate existence. These people may reinvigorate their marriages with energy, though usually only after a good deal of soul-searching, followed by bitter and prolonged confrontation.

The effect that an affair will have on a marriage is devilishly hard to predict. It's not common, but sometimes affairs stabilize a marriage that is dependent on emotional distance. The spouse who wants to be left alone may look the other way when there are signs of infidelity. He (or she) wants a great deal of independence and freedom, so when she (or he) has an affair, that balances the relationship. Even these arrangements, however, are unlikely to be stable. Lovers tire of coming second; some let go, others tighten their grip and demand that their partner get a divorce.

Affairs usually involve emotional inequality, especially when one person is married and the other is not. The married person wants to limit the relationship; the lover wants more. The same disparity can apply when both parties are married, because one is likely to be more committed to marriage than the other. Women, more than men, are apt to be victimized in this situation. Sadly common are cases, like the following, where a woman leaves her husband and then waits in vain for the lover to leave his wife.

When Claudia fell in love with another man after several years of marriage, the poverty of her marriage became all too apparent. Her lover was successful, attentive, open to feelings—oh yes, and married. But being with him made her feel worthwhile again. His marriage was also unhappy, so they talked about getting divorced and married to each other. In the meantime, they both consulted psychotherapists to help them resolve their troubled feelings.

Claudia left her husband within weeks of starting psychotherapy, not because she had worked through her conflict, but because being in treatment gave her the support she needed to follow her heart. Now she was free to be alone with her lover whenever she wanted. Only it turned out not to be whenever she wanted. He couldn't always get away. He said he loved her; he said his marriage was bankrupt, but he didn't seem able to leave. "Give me time," he pleaded, and she did.

Her friends told her she was crazy—"He'll never leave his wife"—but she knew better. In a way she was right; he did love her, perhaps as much as she loved him. The difference was he couldn't bring himself to suffer the humiliation and condemnation he expected from a divorce. He had planned to leave, but as time went on, he wanted to stay married and have a mistress.

Claudia couldn't let go even when it became clear that he was not going to leave his wife. This, unhappily, is not an unusual situation. But that is cold comfort for a woman who gives everything to a man and gets only half of him in return. Claudia's lover, the man who couldn't leave his wife, may try to drag out the affair, but in time he is likely to gravitate back to the security of his marriage.

People with excessively permissive backgrounds may engage in extramarital sex with little or no feeling of shame. Younger members of the baby boom generation developed a freer attitude toward sex in the sixties. Most people, however, feel intense guilt. This may help to explain why most affairs are first and only affairs.

Once they have been unfaithful, many men have an agonizing urge to confess, but fear the consequences. The man's impulse to confess casts him in the role of a naughty child and his wife in the role of an all-forgiving mother. Confession may bring forgiveness, but it is likely to hurt the spouse irredeemably; it may give the person license to be unfaithful again or break up the marriage.

Married women are less likely to confess infidelity, because their husbands are less likely to forgive. A man who discovers his wife "cheating" may fear that it is a reflection on his sexual prowess. (The cuckold is still an object of scorn in our culture.) Since martyrdom isn't considered a desirable male quality, men often react with violence, as though someone had stolen their property.

Whether or not a relationship can withstand infidelity depends on the strength of the couple's bond. Cohabiting couples are in the most jeopardy; without a marriage contract, whatever agreement they have about fidelity is likely to be somewhat vague and open to different interpretations by each partner. Tangible ties, such as children, a joint business, or financial interdependence, keep many couples together. Lacking a strong bond, a relationship may be destroyed by infidelity. A one-night stand is not necessarily serious, but the consequences are impossible to predict. Infidelity confessed may produce a crisis that eventually brings the couple closer. On the other hand, a person who has been unfaithful and honest risks losing the partner's trust forever from a single indiscretion.

Glorification of asocial individualism has undermined the sense of duty to family. When family ties are seen as something external—and optional—many people feel them only as restraint. Some submit, while others rebel. Their own needs frighten them; the needs of their families appall them. Caught in what feels like a trap, many people dream of romantic love and think of it as the way out.

Some people have always known their marriages weren't satisfying; others only discover what's been missing after an extramarital affair. The sexual passion they uncover is so blinding that they pursue it with little thought to the consequences for the family. For those who agonize over the decision to go or stay, the issue boils down to whether or not they can take the risk to emancipate themselves. Often the fate of the family hangs in the balance between guilt and passion. Leaving breaks up the family; staying is for many people like taking bitter medicine—they only do it because they "have to."

Divorce

Of course, a lot of midlife crises do end in divorce. Often with good reason, sometimes with good results. Some people aren't meant to live together and are happier apart. As for the children, they may be better off with parents living separately in peace than together at war. It isn't divorce that determines the children's adjustment; it is the nature of their parents' relationship, with or without divorce. Still, we worry more about the children than we do about their parents. Children are small, they need the family; parents are grown up, they don't. Or do they?

Psychologist Mavis Hetherington recently studied the psychological impact of divorce on the lives of forty-eight men, observed for two years after they divorced. Middle-aged men are often assumed to profit from divorce at their wives' and children's expense. Men, so this thinking goes, escape from responsibility; women and children lose, financially and emotionally. Hetherington and her colleagues found that one-third of fathers reported an excited sense of freedom immediately following divorce; but this feeling alternated with, and by one year was replaced by, depression, anxiety, or apathy.

The pain of the divorced father is worse than he anticipated. Because he lives in another house, or even another city, he can no longer share the everyday pleasure of watching his children grow up. He may console himself with the notion of "quality time," but there is no substitute for being there. He can arrange special activities for his visits—roller skating, trips to the zoo, movies, pizza parlors—but you can't program "meaningful" conversation. Kids tend to talk seriously only when it's their idea. That usually occurs spontaneously, in the midst of everyday routine. A child may be helping dad mow the law, when out comes, "Daddy, what's dope?" or "Were you afraid to ask girls out when you were sixteen?"

Guilt and distance combine to cause divorced fathers to doubt their moral authority. They wonder, will the children hate them for the rest of their lives? This makes them hesitant to discipline the children during their precious time together and hasty in reaching for their checkbooks. They want to believe that they are good fathers, even from across town. What hurts is knowing that when they are needed they may not be there.

By the end of two years the men in Hetherington's study complained of feeling shut out, rootless, and at loose ends. Most of them yearned for an intimate, loving, stable heterosexual relationship.

Middle-aged men who do remarry after a divorce generally choose women who are quite young. The man may be rejuvenated by love with a younger woman, but may discover later that he has only traded one set of problems for another. If divorce were merely getting away from a bad situation, then it might work. But if it is running away from a fear of intimacy, it seldom solves the problem.

The plight of divorced women is now a familiar story, but it is no less catastrophic. Once, divorce meant poverty, stigma, and loneliness. Divorced women today often feel like losers or failures, but now divorce is so common that the stigma is considerably less. That leaves poverty and loneliness.

Since 1980, forty-one states have had equitable distribution laws, which replaced the common-law principle of awarding property to the spouse who held title to it. This means that even though the house and the car are in the husband's name, these assets are to be divided equitably at divorce. The new laws have also done away with the concept of alimony, replacing it with "maintenance"—a temporary award to help the financially dependent partner get reestablished.

Unfortunately, the new laws have not changed the fact that most divorces are financially devastating for women. The new statutes are sufficiently vague that what is "equitable" requires a good deal of discretionary judgment. In an adversarial legal system, the judgment often favors the spouse with the assets—the "deep pocket" as he is known among matrimonial lawyers—who can afford to hire the best attorneys and divulge as little information as possible.

Although joint custody has become more common in the eighties, in the overwhelming majority of cases mothers get the children. Along with the children, they also get child support. Or they are supposed to. Eighty percent of the divorced mothers in American receive no child support, whether it was mandated by the courts or not. Democratic representative Barbara Kennelly of Connecticut calls child support "a national disgrace." Of the 4.5 million women legally entitled to such support, Kennelly found that fewer than half receive the full amount awarded to them. Divorce means permanent poverty for a large number of women and their custodial children. And it doesn't take long to happen. According to Lenore Weitzman, a sociologist at Stanford, a woman's standard of living falls by an average of 73 percent in the year following a divorce, while a man's *rises* by 42 percent.

Even when a woman instigates divorce to get out from under an intolerable marriage, things may not turn out as planned. The freedom and excitement of being single soon palls when a woman discovers that it's hard to meet eligible men over thirty-five. Life after divorce may be lonely for men as well, but the ratio of free heterosexual men to women makes it much easier for men to find new love in midlife.

Fearing the effect of divorce on their young children, many people delay divorce until the children are old enough to withstand the shock. Often the timing involves the midlife adults' financial and career status as well as the age of the children. Some women wait until they have some hope of financial security before announcing their intention to leave. Men sometimes use a transfer as the occasion to leave their troubled marriages. When divorce is planned, the calculations focus on finances and the children. Missing from the usual equation is a recognition that husband and wife may need each other, "for better or worse."

Divorce may, and often does, have unanticipated destructive impact. We all know people in bad marriages. Some couples are grossly mismatched in intelligence, interests, and background; others seem to fight all the time. Still, a surprising number of people seem to fall apart after leaving what looked like disastrous marriages. From the perspective of my clinical experience, the outcome of divorce is hard to predict. When couples ask me whether or not they should divorce, I thank God it's not my decision.

Normal Reactions: Constructive or Compensatory?

Many courses of action at midlife seem to be constructive but are really compensatory. A solution is compensatory when, instead of resolving a problem, it offers a defensive substitute as a counterbalance. Compensatory solutions are devoted to rearranging external circumstances; they involve some activity that is pursued to excess and if interrupted leaves the person intensely anxious. Most attempted solutions fall into one of two categories: "more of the same" or diversionary. Thus we see legions of adults who frantically accelerate their efforts to be successful at love or work, while others turn their energies toward leisure activities, pursued with the passion of a crusade.

There is nothing wrong with striving for success. Working hard to achieve what we want, whether it is a noble contribution to humanity or a grand house with a swimming pool, is part of what makes life rewarding. One oil company executive, who earned $217,000 in 1985, said, "Compensation is an acknowledgment of one's place in the race." A sense of mastery may be a more important measure of success than material rewards. Any trade, profession, or occupation can provide deep satisfaction and a sense of meaning. Making a living at a job that is also intrinsically satisfying is one element in a common formula for successful living.

The problem occurs when we become obsessed with achievement itself, as though it were the only thing that matters. The office is not a good substitute for life itself. Nor is devotion to work a cure for feeling insignificant and unloved. For many people, success provides temporary immunity from insecurity only as long as they climb one step higher. There are many prizes for success, but love and self-fulfillment may not be among them. This simple truth is elusive because it always seems as though the next achievement will bring peace—and there is always one more after that.

One college professor was so preoccupied with winning the teaching award, completing a major research project, and getting tenure that her marriage fell apart. She had no intention of neglecting her family, but she put them on hold until success on the job was assured. Unfortunately, the family couldn't wait.

A computer executive worked seven days a week, hoping to reach the corporate hierarchy. His wife didn't like not having him home, but was willing to be wife, mother, *and* father in order to share in the eventual success. Unfortunately, this man was not promoted to district manager because he lacked the temperament of an administrator. His secret fears were then confirmed, and he thought he was empty and worthless. (Success may not have made him whole but, like going to see the Wizard of Oz, it's hard to give up the illusion of fulfillment as long as the promise beckons in the distance.) It took a painful period of depression and a long reassessment before he adjusted his sights to a job that fit the talents he did have.

Another man, a lawyer, was unhappy at home and at work. At home, he found it hard to accept his wife's independent interests and personal friends. He felt insecure; he acted mean and jealous. The problem, he thought, was that he had too little status and challenge at work. If he could feel better about himself he wouldn't worry so much about her. As a junior partner in an established firm, he was delegated routine cases, with little chance either to show what he could do or to bring in large fees. Rationalizing that if only he could hold his head up at work, he would feel secure at home, he quit the firm and started his own company. He did succeed. No longer was he preoccupied with his lack of status, but his obsession with success only grew stronger. Now he saw less and less of his wife. The marriage slowly deteriorated from his lack of involvement, but it was a long time before he noticed.

Careerism swallows life. The consuming commitment to work leaves little capacity for full participation in leisure pursuits or family life. There are only twenty-four hours in a day, and those people who spend most of them at work may not have much to give at home. Workaholics used to be mainly men, but the single-minded pursuit of career success is now apparent among women, who are beginning to rise to high-level jobs in significant numbers.

Men and women who wear themselves out at work are unlikely to spend their weekends mowing the lawn or playing with the kids. When a man gives his all to his career, his marriage suffers, yet it is likely to survive. When a married woman devotes her self to a career, the marriage may not last. The man who marries his career may never be more than a peripheral husband and father, but our culture accepts, almost expects, a man to think mainly about his work. We (and he) expect his wife to be the guardian of the relationship.

In their authoritative study of *American Couples,* Philip Blumstein and Pepper Schwartz found that "unhappiness and conflict over the way jobs intrude into the relationship are often associated with a couple's breakup." But, "it is primarily the woman's job that is at issue. We find that when a husband gets upset about his wife's job, even in established relationships, the marriage is more likely to fail." When a married woman resumes her career she is likely to find that her husband resists changing the traditional pattern. A young woman who makes a similar commitment to her career may not get married at all. One of the defining groups of the eighties are those young career-oriented, professional women who are rising up in the nation's urban centers.

Rosemary is a legislative assistant for a powerful member of Congress. She is single, but not by choice. She never made a deliberate choice to remain single or even to delay getting married; she simply decided to become the best lawyer she could be. In law school, she dated, but didn't allow herself the time to get serious with anyone. Later, when she went to Washington, she was still interested in meeting men, but didn't have time to make a project out of it. Now, at thirty-seven, she is doing the most important work of her life, drafting legislation on consumer safety. She thinks about having a baby, but the demands of her career are such that she may not be able to fit it in.

Another woman looked forward to enjoying her own interests, including gardening and pottery, after her children left home for school. It wasn't long, though, before she felt that she needed to make a different kind of contribution, and so she went back to school to get a degree in social work. After years of giving her all to her husband and children, she made a 180-degree shift, throwing all her energy into the new vocation. Following graduation, she set up her own practice and she was fairly successful. It was during this period that she consulted me. "Why," she wondered, "when I have finally made something of myself, do I feel so empty?" I had my own ideas, but before we could explore the problem in any depth, she decided that if her career was not fulfilling, the answer must be to make more money and achieve more status. Her solution was to return to school, and so she commuted to New York City in order to study at a prestigious psychoanalytic institute. Her initial success wasn't satisfying; maybe more would be.

Some of these people succeeded and some didn't; but whether they did or not had little bearing on solving their dilemmas. The major factor in whether or not the midlife crisis is resolved is the degree to which dreams of accomplishment are still pursued as solutions to unresolved personal problems. The unconscious assumption is that once we achieve success we will feel loved and secure. "Once I make vice president (get my master's degree, or whatever), people will admire me; no one will criticize me, and I'll be loved"—or so we think.

The Cult of Fitness

Other people, lacking the drive or opportunity for professional success, concentrate on the hours after work, pouring their energy into programs of self-improvement, hobbies, and sports. According to psychologist Michael Mahoney, single people are especially likely to be busy with self-improvement, either seeking to be more appealing to potential partners or trying to make up for the lack of intimate companionship. Married people take up hobbies to give themselves a chance to be by themselves or to have something to do together. Some people dabble in leisure activities; others pursue them doggedly, as though sitting still might drive them crazy. Among the most popular activities of the eighties are tennis lessons, folk dancing, guitar lessons, sailing and photography classes, courses in computer programming, Chinese cooking, car repair instruction, group bicycle trips, and fixing up antique furniture. The real middle-age mania of the eighties, however, is physical fitness.

Sports offers one of the purest forms of release and escape from everyday reality. Unlike sex and alcohol, there are no hangovers or emotional complications. The fantasies and challenges of athletics can be freely adjusted and need not require the cooperation of other people. Men in our culture are imbued with associations between sports and virile achievement. I know at least a dozen middle-aged men who didn't make the football team in high school, but admit to a sense of masculine pride at taking up some form of robust physical activity in midlife. The forty-year-old jogger with no hope of running a four-minute mile can chase six minutes as the symbol of success. Sport also satisfies the need for physical exertion and renews the sense of youthfulness and vigor.

The propaganda of physical fitness stresses the contribution to health and longevity—this makes it okay to play. Mom's daily three-mile run "takes care of her health" and makes the activity more legitimate. Play is a form of regeneration without the same risk as tampering with the critical structures of love and work. Moreover, just as the challenges of sport are tangible, so are the reassuring satisfactions of getting back in shape and keeping up with younger people.

Sport for women takes on the added meaning of throwing off "feminine" reticence. Women now compete with men for space at the local Nautilus center. What's wrong with that? There is nothing wrong with health-inducing exercise and no reason why men should have a monopoly on the pleasure of exercising their bodies. Lifting weights is fine, but spending hours in the gym will not overcome a woman's inner feelings of weakness—any more than it will a man's.

Ours is a health-conscious society, with programs of self-improvement vying with traditional forms of entertainment for popular consumption. One of the reasons for the phenomenal success of professional tennis is that so many adults are now participants as well as spectators. In the late 1970s and early 1980s, health and exercise clubs sprang up like mushrooms after a summer shower. And everywhere you look you see people running.

People of all ages are now actively participating in sports and recreations that were once the exclusive province of the young. Swimming has become popular with the elderly; middle-aged adults are now playing racquetball and other highly strenuous sports; even kids are running marathons. Age is no longer the determining factor in who participates and who sits on the sidelines. When you look closely at any of these programs of self-improvement, you will see in the vanguard people in, or just about to enter, the midlife transition.

I myself am a great believer in exercise and other forms of self-enrichment. Twice in my thirties I went back for advanced study at institutes in my field; I have taken courses in typing, statistics, foreign languages, yoga, nutrition, and effective teaching; and I have been an active participant in football, basketball, tennis, swimming, soccer, weight lifting, and running. I have always done these things, and I plan to continue. But . . . it's possible to confuse invigorating refreshment with life itself. The most common solutions to midlife malaise—diversion in a variety of exercise programs, hobbies, and new projects—are often ways for people to lose, not find, themselves.

Several years ago I became a runner. Earlier, I had retired from sports where you score points, and I felt crummy. My energy level was low, I was twenty pounds overweight, and I smoked five cigars a day. So I took up running.

It wasn't easy. I have the quixotic temperament and impatience of a sprinter (which I was in school). Furthermore, I had tried to run several times unsuccessfully. I put on my sneakers, went out to the street, and sprinted around the block. But I never got as far as a mile before getting winded. My knees ached and I had terrible stitches in my sides. (Runners will recognize that I was going about it all wrong.)

Then my brother, who ran six to eight miles every day, gave me the tip that got me started. Running, he said, is boring and painful until you get used to it. Run slowly; just go as far as you can; but—here's the main thing—run every day for two months, and *then* decide if you like it. Find a regular time, and then run if you feel like it, run if you don't feel like it; run if the weather is good; run if it's raining, snowing, or too hot. Just run every day.

Once I made a commitment—that much-abused word—to run for two months, there was no longer an option to drop out. In the first few weeks everything hurt: knees, calves, heels, lungs; even my arms got heavy. But I had promised myself, so I continued. Before long I could run a mile, then three miles. By that time I was hooked. First came the personal satisfaction of being able to run three miles; then there was the renewed physical sense of well-being. I lost weight, quit smoking, cut way back on drinking, and I felt great.

Someone suggested I enter a race, but I was reluctant. I didn't want my own personal demon—competition—to ruin the simple joy of running. Eventually, though, I picked a ten-kilometer race, which was a great motivation since it was two miles longer than my previous record. The race was terrific! There were so many people that I could merge myself in the company of others, taking heart from the fact that so many were climbing the same hills and enduring the same heat. But the best part was that I had absolutely no sense of wanting to win or even to beat anybody. I just wanted to run my own race.

I found that races gave me incentive to keep running and gradually to extend the distance. Soon I, who once could not run a mile, was running ten.

Running through my first winter toughened me up considerably. It gets cold in New England, and I chose to do my running in the morning darkness. I learned that I could run on dark mornings even when the temperature was well below zero. What made it possible was that, in my mind, there was no option. Deciding to do something when you don't feel like it is often harder than doing it. Each morning when I got out of bed, I had to face the cold, dark wind. But I didn't have to face the sleepy voice who tried to convince the rest of me to stay in bed; I refused to give him a chance to speak.

Like a lot of novice runners, when I first heard about the marathon it seemed like an impossible distance: twenty-six miles is a long way in the car—how can anybody run that far? But with some encouragement from a friend in the local running club, I decided to try it. My friend helped me plan a crash course that he said would enable me to finish a marathon in three months. Finishing, he added, was the only sensible goal for a first marathon. Most experts agree that in order to complete a marathon on your feet the minimum training is three months of running about fifty miles per week. So that's what I did. Another secret is to put in two or three long runs of about twenty miles in the weeks preceding the race. I did that too. Running twenty miles gave me a tremendous sense of confidence. If I could run twenty, surely I could finish the last six when I had to. Experienced runners say that the halfway point in a marathon comes at twenty miles, but I was sure they were exaggerating.

I soon discovered the truth about twenty miles being only half the battle. When I reached the twenty-mile mark in the race, I was exhausted but still running. Beyond that point I slipped into a twilight state, like nothing I'd ever felt before. Everything ached. *Everything.* With each step I had to overcome the agonizing sensation that comes when your system has used up its supply of glycogen. But thinking about crossing the finish line kept me going. I tried to imagine how happy and proud I would be, and I kept running—well, moving. Finally, the finish line appeared, but there was no joy, just relief.

My second marathon was much easier, and I was much faster. A trained runner's body adjusts to the need to burn fuel over a prolonged distance, and the agony of the first time is not usually repeated. Now that I could do it, I wanted to do it faster. My first marathon took three hours and forty-five minutes; my second took only three hours and nine minutes. I still had no interest in beating other people, but I did want to beat myself. So I started training hard. I ran as many as eighty miles a week and also worked out with weights and did speed work on the track. Some of my friends suggested that I was doing too much—"Look how thin you are!"—but I knew better. I was accomplishing something.

I didn't figure out what was going on until later, and I didn't exactly slow down on purpose. My publisher wanted me to finish a book I was working on a lot sooner than I had planned. I had to cut way back on my running and promised myself it was only temporary. But by the time I delivered the manuscript I realized that running had become the primary focus of my life. It was probably good for me, but I had overdone it. Thinking it over, I decided that if I put some of that energy into my career and my family, the rewards would be greater. It wasn't really a matter of time, but of priorities. Today I still run, but it is once again *my* race, more recreation than obsession.

Looking back, I think that my running was part of an adaptive response to the early warnings of a midlife crisis. At that time I was struggling with self-doubt about my career and finding it difficult to adjust to life with two demanding infants. Running paid off directly and indirectly. For me, engaging in a joyful physical activity was a wonderful release—even better for the soul than for the body. Moreover, the self-discipline that I discovered through running was applicable to other parts of my life as well. I remember thinking how difficult an upcoming meeting at work would be, when it suddenly dawned on me, "Hell, if I can run ten miles, I can certainly stand up and say what needs to be said."

During the period of my intense running, I did what I felt

I had to at work and at home. I became director of the clinic where I worked. I also became a pretty good father, often making up with special weekend outings for my long absences during the workweek. In both of these areas of my life, however, I think I was stuck at a plateau of development. The pleasure of running helped distract me from this realization, and the hours it consumed helped perpetuate the impasse. Because I am a private, solitary person, running was particularly well-suited to help me avoid overcoming problems with intimacy. I was a workaholic who turned to running with the same single-minded preoccupation I had once applied to my career. Today, I am aware of my own tendency to shift from one preoccupation to another—say, from running to writing. But I am also aware that my own life is richest when I bring diversity to it and keep things in proportion.

Exercise and sports produce a healthy affirmation of the physical side of life. When pursued to excess, however, a regressive shift in priorities takes place. I say regressive because there is a retreat from the main business of adult life. The impulse behind the retreat is to move from complicated tasks to simpler ones, where control is largely in your own hands. Most people feel that their success at work and happiness at home is mediated by others. The average worker blames the boss or "the system" for lack of career achievement and satisfaction. Husbands blame wives, wives blame husbands, and both of them blame the children for domestic disappointment. "There's nothing *I* can do," one patient complained; "the bureaucracy makes it impossible for me to do my job right." The same man had long ago given up trying to talk with his wife, because "She's never going to change; what's the use?"

Sports and games become a problem when the rest of life is neglected; when the competitive mania for winning takes over the spirit of playful enjoyment; or, as often happens, when the recreation becomes a compulsion. Weekend athletes are acutely sensitive to this charge—just as practitioners of more traditional forms of worship are sensitive to psychological interpretations of their motivation. Sports are worthwhile, not only because they build healthy bodies, but because they bring joy and zest. They do provide healthy physical exercise, but more important, they should be a source of playful fantasy and an expression of pleasure.

Many people, facing a midlife reassessment, undertake sports as personal and social therapy or as an ersatz solution to feelings of inner emptiness and emotional isolation. These people run, not for joy, but to shore up a faltering sense of self. In a nation of idol worshippers, narcissistic dreams of fame and glory are personified by celebrities of sport. These dreams of adulation die hard, because they are formed early in life and never critically examined. The weekend athlete is often playing out the role of a youthful dream. The child wanted to be as loved and admired as, say, Mickey Mantle or Wilma Rudolph; the adult runs five miles a day and enters local road races.

A fast-rising I.B.M. executive once told me, "Running a marathon at age thirty-eight was the proudest achievement of my life." His story illustrates that compulsive recreation and career success are not mutually exclusive; but, in his case at least, the hours spent running were also spent running away from an unhappy family life.

One of the many ends that compulsive leisure pursuits serve is as distractions that shield parents from daily emotional involvement with their children. Many husbands abandon their children to the wives whose company they find uninteresting, while they go out running. But some middle-aged runners are like hamsters on a treadmill: running keeps them busy, but doesn't break down the walls of their cages.

"Thirty-Nine and Holding"

Not everyone worries about dying, drinks too much, has an affair, or takes up vigorous exercise; but most of the people I know deal with these issues in one way or another—they think about them, work hard to deny them, or maybe wonder if their spouses are going through some kind of crisis. Does everyone have a midlife crisis? I don't know. But I do know this: I have never discussed the subject with anyone who has a neutral attitude about it. People either identify the signs of crisis in their own experience or vigorously deny that they ever felt uneasy or made readjustments at midlife.

Age forty often seems to confront us before we are ready. Those who protest too loudly—the "thirty-nine and holding" syndrome—become figures of fun. To avoid their fate we try to adjust, adapt, and accommodate—terms that suggest settling for life as you find it.

Resignation means knowing that things aren't as good as they might be, but deciding to put up with them anyway. Some people mistake established and routinized modes of behavior for what is natural and healthy. If they have always been a little bored or a little lonely, they think that's the way life is. That is all some people expect—and that's all they get. Those who opt for resignation learn to blunt their sensitivities. They either keep themselves from becoming aware of signals to change or wrestle their feelings into submission as soon as they surface, and retreat into a pattern of resigned acquiescence, often rationalized as "maturity."

Unsettled American society in the 1980s accentuates our craving for security. Today, it is difficult to change, difficult to move around; selling houses and buying houses, and looking for work—these are always hard; today they are harder. Above all we seem to want daily life to be reliable, safe, predictable. We withdraw from avenues of potential satisfaction to avoid conflict over our desires and the hard work to bring them to fruition.

However, middle age is not an affliction that we must resign ourselves to. True, we are getting older; true, we need to accept certain limitations in ourselves and in the world around us; but fatalistic resignation and ceasing to develop are false requisites to maturity.

It is almost inevitable to feel discouraged somewhere along in midlife. As survival needs recede, the needs for pleasure and fulfillment reemerge. We have spent years coming into our own, developing our talents, our unique gifts, learning to bear disappointments, becoming mature, seasoned, so that we can stand with some dignity. Despite all that we've done, though, happiness evades us.

Of course, there is always the bitter consolation of regret. This is perhaps more common in late life, but for many people it begins much earlier. "Ah, if I were only seventeen again, with my whole life before me." "If only," many of us pine, we had completed a degree, married so-and-so, stayed single, worked harder at that first job, quit before we were earning so much money, bought a house before the interest rates went through the ceiling, and so on, and on . . .

Why do so many people opt for resignation as a way of life? Some are convinced that the forces affecting their lives are too powerful to change; others see where they could make changes, but are afraid. In fact, many of us are all too ready to believe that if we can't make significant changes, we are "weak," "cowardly," or "neurotic." Such mental flagellation only serves to deter us from further understanding of why we behave as we do *and* helps us avoid doing something about it.

Sometimes I think there are two kinds of people. One group is weak, cowardly, and neurotic; they find change difficult and give up. The second group is weak, cowardly, and neurotic; they find change difficult, but do it anyway.

The Window to Renewal

What are the symptoms of stagnation? At work, we forfeit personal meaning and a sense of achievement when we choose security over satisfaction. Bitterness gives rise to a devaluation of work. Some people feel like losers. In others, their own sense of failure fuels a mean-spirited reaction to those around them. The resulting isolation only makes things worse.

Chronic, sullen anger also poisons family life. The family, which should be an emotional sanctuary, is felt as an oppressive burden. The root of these feelings may be inside ourselves, but most of us don't dare to look there. Real pleasure—the kind that comes from devotion to a vocation, from rewarding family relations, and from deep friendship—is often blocked by inner and outer restraints. Overcoming these blocks means taking a hard look at ourselves and our relations with others, and renewing our commitment to life.

The pain of crisis is the window to renewal. Renewal is a resurrection of unused potential. It means taking up again the program of self-discovery that we put aside so many years ago. Now, in midlife, we can unfreeze fixed images of ourselves and fixed habits of living. We can discover untapped reservoirs of power to enjoy life with a higher level of meaning and satisfaction.

I'm not talking about some ephemeral perfection—the pursuit of "self-actualization"—that dooms us always to fall short. I'm talking about a practical reevaluation that results in an affirmation of life. Translated into action, this means becoming more secure in ourselves and more able to enjoy loving relationships with others.

5

The Mind in Conflict

MIDLIFE has inherent stresses, affecting nearly all of us in one way or another. But these conscious vexations do not fully explain our anxiety and pessimism. The fact that some people have more trouble than others with the idea of turning forty makes it hard to overlook the role of individual differences in adjustment. While it may be convenient to blame one's unhappiness on turning forty, I regret to say there is not much justification for this. The longing to break away, the frustrated need for reassurance, and the fear of life itself—these are not the result of turning forty. These are the distillates of earliest experience, and they surface when stress reactivates the conflicts of the past.

In adolescence and early adulthood, we learned to navigate the world in ways that satisfied some of our needs while compensating for some of our shortcomings. We managed to function well enough so long as swings of self-doubt and self-acceptance were within normal limits. At the same time, pivotal problems often remained submerged, not resolved.

Much of what we hide from ourselves is projected onto others, often our spouses. Marriage is a union not only of two separate people, but also of two interlocking sets of needs and expectations. The groom looks at his young bride and sees the embodiment of all his desires. Later, when they quarrel, he sees his mother standing there. Perhaps she also sees what she wants to see: a man much older and wiser than he is, or at least strong enough not to need a mother. Some of these expectations are rudely frustrated in the early years of marriage. But some fictions are lived out in a collusive process of mutual distortion. Over the years, couples seem to grow alike in some ways, while polarizing each other in certain critical areas.

In addition to relatively conscious expectations, each partner also brings a residue of unintegrated, unconscious attitudes. Frightening forces of love and hate, buried deep in the psyche, are disinterred in the marriage. Some of these abhorred qualities are externalized onto the spouse, who becomes a distorted personification of disowned impulses and restraints: the man who works long hours to earn money for luxuries "because his wife is materialistic" may be acting out his own greed without having to face it; the corporate lawyer who leaves work to stay home with her children "because her husband is old-fash-ioned" may avoid working through her own conflict between competitiveness and nurturance.

When the barriers that obstruct us seem senseless, it's com-forting to have a scapegoat. Consider the example of a man who was stuck as a big success in a small job.

After several years in the sales force of a large corporation, he moved up to become a division manager. At first the job was challenging. He had to learn to give orders without giving offense, and he had to learn to coordinate his own efforts with those of other division heads. Ten years later he was comfortable, but he knew it was time to move on. There were plenty of openings for new managers, yet somehow he never put his name in.

The problem, he said, was his wife. "She won't move." She liked the neighborhood, she liked the neighbors, and she made no secret of it. But she'd move; she had done so before and she was prepared to do so again. Only in his mind was she inflexible. He promoted her minor reservations into a staunch refusal. He felt trapped and controlled by her, but it was easier than facing the truth. As long as he could blame her for being reluctant to relocate, he did not have to confront his own fear of competing at a higher level.

It may not matter how the partner actually behaves; evidence contrary to expectation is easily distorted—perception shapes reality as needs dictate. Over the years, the spouse may actually become the incarnation of unwanted characteristics. The longer one person is perceived in a starkly rigid fashion, the more he or she comes to personify the fixed view. Gradually, internal conflicts of two, once separate individuals are played out across the blurred boundary of the marital relationship. Otherwise intolerable aspects of the self are not simply projected—attributed to the partner—but the partner takes on the projected role. She becomes the shrew he needed to justify feeling victimized; he becomes the irresponsible child she needs to repudiate.

Prohibitions and restraints make up much of what is passed off to the spouse. "If it weren't for her, I could be out having fun with my friends." "If it weren't for him, I wouldn't be stuck at home with these kids." One-dimensional cultural stereotypes reinforce these beliefs. Men who are too shy to

socialize and women who are afraid to assert their independence comfort themselves with the illusion that it is all her—
or his—fault. If they ever discover that the fearful inhibitions
are in their own minds, they have a chance to come to terms
with them, leaving them free to work out their own fates *and*
to be more at ease with their real partners.

The Hidden Self

While the cause of our problems may not lie in external circumstances, the nature of these provides clues to the inner
problems. What is it that so troubles people about turning
forty? Men complain most about meaningless drudgery on
their jobs and routine in their family lives. Women are likely
to regret years given over to self-sacrifice. The unhappy result
is anxiety and low-grade depression; and conflict, usually revolv-
ing around gratification versus duty. Feelings such as these
expose nuclear personality traits tied to early experience. The
more the trait is structurally embedded in the personality, the
earlier the experience.

Many people doubt the prepotent influence of early life
experiences because they are remote in memory. Sometimes
it's easier to recognize in others what we cannot see in ourselves. We are all familiar with grownups who withdraw or fly
into a rage when they get angry—these are the most troubled
of our acquaintances. People who are this frozen in childhood
patterns have problems all their lives; midlife may be hard for
them, but so is every other part of life. Others, who first have
trouble in midlife, were more successful at negotiating the
earlier stages. With these people the metaphor of being frozen
into childhood patterns doesn't work. These people are not
frozen in the past; they got beyond that. But they didn't resolve

critical developmental problems. Instead, they suppressed them. Residual problems can be avoided for years and only surface under pressure. To understand what lies beneath, we need a psychology of depth.

There are two particularly useful models of depth psychology: the classical Freudian theory of conflict and the emerging psychology of the self, conceived by Heinz Kohut. Stripped of their jargon, these theories maintain that midlife anxieties signal the reemergence of unresolved childhood fears and uncover the precariousness of the basic sense of self. Each of these theories describes emotional vulnerabilities that make us afraid to grab hold of life. As long as we carry around these inner liabilities we cannot function with all of life's juices. When we're afraid of full commitment to love or work, we operate at half-speed.

The basic idea of Freudian psychology is that human passions are tamed by cultural restraints. In youth, our animal nature is domesticated; unfortunately, some of us are overly domesticated. Instead of being spurred on by our drives, we are shackled by anxiety and guilt. According to conflict theory, we are in perpetual struggle between sexual and aggressive impulses on the one hand and fear of punishment on the other. Even as little children, we began to discover that the life force, or "libido," is considered dangerous and must be subdued. Our desires seem to be the cause of our problems with our parents. "Good" (compliant and complaisant) children don't get into trouble; "bad" (assertive and passionate) children do. The result is a fear of desire.

Incidentally, we need not restrict our view of people as driven solely by sexual desire to accept psychoanalytic thinking; "libido" embraces all that is involved in the need for personal relationships. The mechanisms of inner conflict are spelled out in psychoanalytic structural theory, according to which personality is guided by competing interests; the mind is in conflict and behavior is an uneasy synthesis of contradictory promptings.

The Mind in Conflict

Freud's experience with neurotic patients convinced him that the crucial determinant of psychological maladjustment was whether or not certain contents of the mind were accessible to consciousness. Initially he thought that the critical elements were unconscious memories of traumatic events, especially molestation in childhood; later he concluded that the memories were a product not of real events but of wishes for pleasurable gratification. These wishes were repressed because they conflicted with moral standards and mature goals. As long as the fantasies remained unconscious they could give rise to neurotic disturbance; as soon as they were made conscious the neurotic symptoms would disappear.

We are left with a model of personality as a bundle of dichotomies: conscious/unconscious, sex/aggression, and instinct/repression. In this model the psychoanalyst is a detective, ferreting out the secrets of the unconscious, healing by revealing concealed wishes.

These observations formed the basis of Freud's depth model of the mind, articulated in *The Interpretation of Dreams*, which divides the psyche into conscious, preconscious, and unconscious domains. This model was consistent with turn-of-the-century neurology, which recognized a stratification of neurological functioning. According to this thinking, older and more primitive areas of the brain, such as the brain stem, are controlled and suppressed by newer ones like the cortex. The deepest layer in Freud's model, the unconscious, is a repository for instinctual sexual and aggressive wishes striving for discharge; it is a realm where neither logic nor reality prevails; instead ominpotent fantasy reigns supreme. Because these raw wishes are dangerous, defense mechanisms bar the gate to consciousness. This theory seemed to satisfy the prime requisite of a theory of the mind: it offered a satisfactory explanation of emotional conflict. Conflict exists because unconscious sexual wishes are opposed by conscious perceptions of reality and morality.

In a recent controversy over the seduction theory, Jeffrey Masson accused Freud of distorting the reality of neglect and abuse in childhood, falsely blaming his patients for concocting stories of seductions that had actually taken place. Unfortunately, the valid point in Masson's argument gets lost in his overblown and sensationalistic account *(The Assault on Truth)*. Freud did back away from fully exploring the impact of actual relations between parents and children, and modern analysts have neglected the significance of the interpersonal relationships of adulthood. But the controversy over the seduction theory misses the point. The validity of psychoanalysis does not rest with establishing what did or did not happen; as we shall see, Freud moved from a theory of the past—trauma or wishes —to a theory of the present—ongoing conflict in the mind.

Another, more telling, criticism of Freud's thinking has to do with his treatment of women. Unfortunately, psychoanalytic theory has suggested that a woman's role is dictated by her anatomy. Freud was so preoccupied with raw animal drives that he overlooked the primal nature of social forces, especially the cultural conditioning of his own patriarchal society. His psychology of women reveals most clearly the limits of reducing human encounters to biological transactions.

In the phallic stage (around the third year of life) a little girl, according to Freud, discovers that boys have penises and she does not. This discovery shapes her whole life. From that time onward she is envious. She perceives that she has been deprived and feels a permanent sense of inadequacy. Her personality is an inevitable result of her biological inferiority, and her only chance for a semblance of wholeness is to acquire a substitute penis in the form of a child.

Until recently women have succumbed to this propaganda passing for science. Some have protested, but often with the secret fear that they were going against nature. Freud did not create the gender role forced on women—his analysis reflected the cultural reality of his day—but neither did he challenge it. The Freudian vision of women as emasculated creatures, promulgated with the full weight of scientific authority, has reinforced their suppression as much as any force in the twentieth century.

The penis, as psychoanalyst Clara Thompson pointed out, is merely a symbol of privilege in a patriarchal society. Women envy men their privilege, not their genitalia. In their restless search for a better life, women who sought to break out of the female stereotype once imitated men. Today, they are aware that equality does not mean sameness. Women of the eighties, searching for self-definition, do not turn to Freud for an interpretation of what they are and can be.

The Structure of Personality

When Freud emended his original thinking, the result was the structural theory of the mind. This theory divides the mind into three groups of functions: instinctual drives, rational thinking, and moral prohibitions. These functions are called mental structures—id, ego, and superego—hence the name, structural theory.

The *id* is made up of instinctual drives, sexual and aggressive, which constantly press for gratification. The *ego* functions to achieve and maintain contact with social reality through sensation, perception, and motor functions. It also mediates between the demands of the id and superego and those of the environment. This involves the capacity to test reality, that is, to distinguish between inner fantasies and outer reality. The ego's crucial characteristic is the ability to delay the id's otherwise unrestrained tendency to discharge; this includes the ability to engage in mental trial actions, what we call thinking. The *superego* consists of ethical ideals and prohibitions, originating in identification with parental standards of morality.

Because these operations are complex, and their interaction and conflicts more complex still, many people oversimplify them, reducing them to little homunculi of the mind. It may be convenient to think of the superego as a harsh judge, the id as a wild beast, and the ego as a wise arbitrator, but it is not quite correct. Although it is harder to do so, we should be aware that these structural terms refer to types of *actions*, not regions of the mind. They are descriptive not anatomical.

Thus the "id" is a way of acting: erotic or aggressive, infantile, irrational, unrestrained, passionate or playful, heedless of consequences, impulsive, self-contradictory, thoroughly egocentric, with a tendency toward immediate unchecked action; and often these actions are performed unconsciously. The actions of "ego" involve restraint and delay, responding in a way that balances the interests of the person as a whole; "ego" refers to virtually the entire realm of conscious mental activity —thinking, planning, remembering—but more as well, including functions of inhibition and defense, which often take place out of awareness. The "superego" refers to judging one's own actions in an irrational, severely harsh way, just as we imagine our parents did. We ordinarily equate superego with "conscience," but it is more than this, because many parental prohibitions and demands rest in our unconscious. (Conscious morality is likely to be more humane, because it is more a rational ego function than a product of the irrational superego.)

According to Freud, all thoughts, feelings, and behavior are the products of interactions among these types of functioning. All actions are the result of conflicting demands of the id, superego, and ego. As mediator of these demands, the ego must also take outside reality into account; thus the ego serves three masters: id, superego, and reality. When conflicts are manifest, there is the possibility of resolution.

For example, if a woman wants to have an affair with a colleague, but thinks that it is wrong, she can choose to go ahead or not. Her temptation puts her in a quandary, but at least the impulse (from the id) is not so alien (to the ego) as to be unthinkable. Her criteria for deciding whether or not to act on the impulse may be in terms of rational consequences (as perceived by the ego) or in terms of unexamined prohibitions (as dictated by the superego.) What makes psychological conflict more interesting—and more troublesome—is that it is often unconscious. But if conflict is unconscious how do we know it is there?

Inner conflict is signaled by unpleasant emotion, especially when it does not fit the circumstances. The panic that some people feel when a spouse goes away on business, the unaccountable sadness caused by a minor setback, these are the signals that something is wrong beneath the surface.

The Meaning of Anxiety

Our first experience of anxiety occurs in infancy as a result of traumatic stimulation or frustration. No one who has ever watched a baby scream can possibly doubt that traumatic anxiety plays a primal role in early development. As Freud noted, there are certain situations that occur in every child's life that are the primary sources of traumatic anxiety. The first of these is the absence of the mother, which to an infant seems as though she is forever lost. The second situation occurs when the parents scold the very young child, which at that moment feels like the loss of their love. The third is the so-called fear of castration—best understood as a Freudian metaphor for severe punishment that renders one powerless—which arises during the Oedipal period. The Oedipus complex, named for Sophocles' Oedipus Rex, who slew his father and wedded his mother, refers to the family romance that takes place when children of about four to six wish to assert exclusive claim on the parent of the opposite sex. This provokes a jealous reaction in the spouse, and the result is the first love triangle. Fearing retaliation from the rival, the child represses his or her desire and adopts parental prohibitions, which form the basis of the superego. The fourth situation of predictable anxiety is the harsh condemnation rendered by one's own superego.

In each of these prototypic danger situations the child is overcome with anxiety. As the child learns that his or her own behavior can bring about these unhappy events, an association is built up between instinctual impulses and these fearful calamities. What children do not know they imagine: "If Mommy yells at me for muddying the floor, maybe she would kill me if she knew I played with myself." What adults half know, they embellish: "If I allow myself to get close to this person, maybe we will be overwhelmed by sexual feelings." In this way, our own instinctual strivings come to be the felt source of danger and anxiety; the enemy is within. Anxiety becomes a signal and a stimulus, which compels the ego to oppose certain wishes. The ego sets up defenses against these wishes because "it" recognizes that the impulses, if gratified, would lead to danger. Such conflicts need not be abnormal or unhealthy; they become so only when exaggerated fears lead to an overly circumscribed life or when defenses are so restrictive that no gratification is allowed.

Most people are familiar with the notion that anxiety can occur along with an unconscious impulse to behave in a sexual or aggressive way, though it is common to think of the *impulse* as the danger, rather than to realize that the danger is some anticipated punishment for acting on the impulse. Nevertheless, many people continue to think of anxiety as simply a matter of conditioning. This approach often confuses the setting in which the anxiety arises as the problem. For example, a man who has an attack of anxiety in a restaurant may develop a fear of restaurants. Such phobic fears are reinforced by the fact that returning to the restaurant is likely to restimulate the anxiety—regardless of what prompted it in the first place.

Experts, too, can reinforce the idea that the problem is a phobia. If the victim of anxiety consults a behavior therapist, the treatment is likely to involve returning to *the scene of* the anxiety, with or without some form of relaxation to make it easier. If the person is really unlucky, he or she may end up with someone who treats anxiety with medication. The result is very likely to be a dependence on medication to handle situations of anxiety, with no attempt to conquer the fear, much less get at its roots.

Left to their own devices, many people treat anxiety with their personal versions of medication, as the following example illustrates.

The first time I saw Rick he was in the process of separating from his wife, after three years of marriage. The marriage had apparently been a mistake from the start, and the decision to separate was mutual. Rick's problem was an almost incapacitating anxiety that moved in as soon as his wife moved out. He was not the sort of person to seek psychotherapy, so he diagnosed his own problem—"midlife crisis"—and applied his own treatment—diet, exercise, and yoga. He lost some weight but not the anxiety. In fact, it became unbearable. He was apprehensive and agitated all day, at times he even felt that he might explode—he thought he was losing his mind. Reluctantly, he went to a therapist. She, too, thought he was losing his mind, and she sent him to me for psychological testing.

His anxiety was indeed extreme, so extreme in fact that he was confused and disorganized—but not crazy. I suggested that he work things out with his therapist, and I sent her a copy of my findings. I didn't hear from either one of them after that.

Five years later Rick called me. When I recognized his name, I was curious to hear what had happened in his previous therapy, and why he wanted to see me now. "This time," he said, "it's my job."

Although I wanted to ask him what happened five years ago, I restrained my curiosity so that he could talk about what was on his mind. I was hoping to hear something about his life that would explain his anxiety, but he was too preoccupied with his symptoms to speak of anything else. He complained endlessly, almost as though he had some secret plan to punish those around him. Accordingly, my first intervention was symptomatic. I taught him to control the symptoms of an anxiety attack—which is almost always characterized by hyperventilation—by making a concerted effort to breathe gently and shallowly; if he still couldn't control the attack, he should breathe into a paper bag until it subsided.

By our next meeting he had the attacks under control and was ready to try to understand what was behind them. He spoke mostly about his job and an impending change that meant a lot to him. He was a high school teacher, popular with the kids, well-liked by other teachers, and consistently rated as outstanding by the principal. Now he was in line for a promotion, to principal or even superintendent of the local school district. He was ready to give up teaching. He felt that he had earned the right to move up, but he worried about asserting his authority in a position of leadership. As a teacher, the lines of authority were clear; he was comfortable with the principal of the school, a woman, and had no problem maintaining control over the children. But he was uncertain about his ability to handle aggression and assertiveness with other men. His associations, as the session ended, were to growing up in a strict household, run by a domineering father.

Rick began the next session by telling me he was angry because "You made me talk about my family, when the problem is my job." Like a lot of people, his solution to conflict with his parents was to distance himself from them in every possible way. But they kept cropping up in his conversation.

"Last night," he said, "I had my weekly phone call from my mother. She is the only one I talk to at all anymore. I promised that I would visit them at Thanksgiving, but I dread it. I wish there was some way out of it. My parents used to upset me a lot, but not so much anymore. Now I just don't have anything to do with them. I used to dread it when my father came home drunk. Their fights were awful. After he finished yelling at her, he'd find something to yell at me for. It didn't matter what I had done, whether I was good or bad; he'd always find something. And it was no good talking back, then he'd really get furious. My sister used to fight with him. She was the rebellious one. Me, I suppressed everything."

Then he interrupted himself: "I don't want to talk about this stuff. Can't you help me get rid of my anxiety?" (Looking outside instead of in, Rick was an anxiety sufferer on his way to becoming a phobic.) I asked him to tell me about the first anxiety attack he could remember. "When did it happen? Where were you? Who were you with, and what was on your mind?"

He thought for a minute, and then got red in the face. "I remember! It was on the plane, coming back from a visit with my parents. I'd had a terrible fight with my father. And then on the plane, I had this overwhelming panic; I thought I was having a heart attack. When I got home I went to see my doctor, who told me it was anxiety and gave me some Valium." "What were you thinking about on the plane?" Silence . . . Then in a rapid burst: "I wanted to kill him, that son of a bitch! He had no right to say those things to me. I'm not a kid anymore; I'm thirty-seven years old!" Then he broke down, sobbing and moaning.

What made this fight with his father different, and far more toxic, was that Rick had tried to fight back. For years he had tolerated his father's bullying. He told himself that his father was a pigheaded tyrant, and there was no sense arguing with him. The truth is that Rick continued to think of himself as a child. He may have been thirty-seven, but long ago he learned to shrink away from conflict.

On this trip home, however, he didn't. Maybe he was beginning to think of himself in a position of leadership. Or maybe he was just sick and tired of letting his father steamroller him. In any case, when his father started his usual litany of complaints, instead of just waiting for the storm to pass, Rick told him he was tired of the nagging. If his father didn't have anything better to say, why didn't he just shut up. At which point, his father exploded, "How dare you speak to me that way!"

On the plane home, the savagery of his father's attack still burned in his ears, and the murderous thoughts that Rick had repressed for so many years surfaced. But no sooner did the fantasy of killing his father begin to take shape than he pushed it away. All that was left was the anxiety, signaling the dangerous impulse that wouldn't stay buried.

Actually Rick had taken the first step toward cure when he confronted his father. Ironically, he thought it was a big mistake, a regrettable "loss of control." Gradually, Rick was able to realize that his father's harsh response didn't mean that angry self-expression is wrong. But this insight had to be worked through. Insight alone cures nothing—unless it leads to action.

As a youngster, Rick put away his anger to get on with his life. Most of us subdue our personal demons as the only apparent way out of human conflict. We have to protect ourselves against the world, and we do this the way any creature would, by shutting off experience and denying our own anxieties. Otherwise we are crippled for action.

Repression is normal. We spare ourselves deep trouble by keeping our minds on the everyday problems of life. In order to function, we constrict the world and ourselves. In the 1970s and 1980s, young adults, strained to their limits trying to keep up with accelerating technology and a declining economy, choked off too much of themselves, ransoming their vitality to pay for their safety.

In midlife, conflicts reemerge when we are stimulated by new passions or undergo changing relations to old ones. The man who channeled all his aggressions into a hard-driving career may be forced to renegotiate his psychic balance if he moves into the role of a senior, charged with helping colleagues, not killing off the competition. The woman whose marriage had been her passion—a passion that had made other passions unnecessary long ago—will likely suffer great inner turmoil if her desire is reawakened outside of marriage, or if the marriage simply turns stale. Those who are even tempted to act on conflicted desires may be tortured with anxiety; those who do act may be punished with depression.

Depression: The Painful Reminder

The idea that anxiety can signal danger is well-known. That depression can also is less obvious. The difference is that anxiety signals a calamity that *might* happen, while depression signals one that has *already* happened. Depression can occur when something in the present brings back an earlier experience of loss of love, severe punishment, or moral condemnation. The example of Rachel illustrates this process.

Rachel didn't intend to have an affair—it just happened. She hadn't even realized how unhappy she was, until she met Rod. An affair wasn't her style, or his. It was more than that anyway. They were in love; neither of them questioned that. The question for Rachel was what to do about her marriage. Confused and guilty, she consulted a psychotherapist.

Once she began to think about it, Rachel realized that there was plenty wrong with her marriage. With Nathan, her husband, lovemaking had never been satisfying, and they never really talked together. Nathan was always ready to tell her about his latest project, but he never seemed interested in what she was doing. After the affair began, Rachel begged Nathan to understand that something was wrong, something was missing. He agreed to take her back if they could resume the marriage as it had been. That is, he wanted her to take care of the house and children and leave him alone.

It was an astonishingly bad relationship. They were ill-matched—he was interested in business and success; she was interested in people and feelings—and they seemed incapable of relating to each other. She tried, he tried, but after two months they agreed to separate. It seemed reasonable; some people are better off apart. Why then did she become so terribly depressed?

Rachel sought the answer where most people do, in current life circumstances, but she couldn't find it. The therapist looked for something in the past, a forgotten calamity of childhood that had somehow been restimulated in the present.

Rachel did not remember her mother well, but thought of her as full of life and a little crazy. Her mother left with another man when Rachel was quite small. She lived for a time with her father, but then he sent her to live on his sister's farm. It was a big change. Aunt Margaret was strict and proper; she had little time for misbehavior, so Rachel was raised by the book —not Dr. Spock's, more like Cotton Mather's.

Rachel was a passionate child, full of energy, full of life. But now she felt abandoned. Her mother had left, and now her father had sent her away. She couldn't help feeling that she had lost her parents because of something she did—or something she was. She became exquisitely tuned to the whims of her aunt. If the price of security was surrender, she would pay it. Anything, she thought, was better than another rejection.

On the surface she became a "good girl," like a tame rabbit. But her passion for life flourished in fantasy. She dreamed of playing in the mud, fighting with her cousins, and running away to visit her mother. Daydreaming gave her something to hang on to, but also burdened her with anxiety and guilt. If she was *really* a good girl, she wouldn't even think these things.

When she was twelve Rachel's fears came true. Her aunt sent her away. Never mind that the move was dictated by practical necessity; to Rachel it only confirmed that she, who had not subdued her daydreams, was unworthy of love.

Rachel spent her teens with her father, a chaste and chastened man whose values were safety and security. He didn't forbid her socializing, but his description of his lost wife as "a social butterfly" served to discourage it. So instead, Rachel excelled in school—that was safe and her father approved. She poured her passion into learning and planned to become a teacher.

Eventually she went off to college, where she did well and was happy. But after graduation, she again became insecure. College was a haven from the anxieties she grew up with; leaving the campus seemed to deprive her of a necessary secure base. She taught for a while and then married Nathan. She didn't realize it, but marriage was her way of retreating from full participation in life. From the start, she chose security over satisfaction.

Nathan's father had built a prosperous business by taking risks and working hard; Nathan took over and kept things going by working hard and *not* taking risks. He offered Rachel security and material comfort. What love she had for him was energized by her need for a safe haven.

Rachel settled into a role—wife and mother—that she created out of her own longings. Being a good wife to Nathan, giving him babies, and then giving them every bit of her energy, she became the "good mother" she had missed. In the process, she skipped the adventure and passion of young adulthood. Although she had repressed the memories of rejection in childhood, she retained the lesson.

On the outside, she seemed content; on the inside she trembled with choked-off feelings and desires. Her anger burst forth once in a while, and she had dreams that would shock a sailor. But for the most part she kept her balance, with a mixture of self-abnegation and substitute satisfactions. The crisis—her affair with Rod—stripped away her structure of defense, laying bare the underside of her personality.

Leaving her husband was a recapitulation of her mother's desertion, and her depression was the punishment—of her mother and herself.

Rachel's therapy took a long time. Like many people, she had a strong investment in maintaining a particular view of herself and her family, and so it took a lot of painful work to reevaluate and expand that view. Where does change take place, in memory, insight, in relations to the therapist, or in "real life"? In Rachel's case, change in one sphere reverberated to others. A year into therapy an incident occurred that catalyzed a series of new understandings. She had asked me to change one of her hours so that she could perform in a dance recital. This innocent request turned out to be full of conflict for Rachel. She was extremely fearful I would retaliate for her failure to conform to my schedule. In the process of discussing this, a series of childhood incidents reemerged in which her aunt had punished Rachel for asserting her wishes. The pictures took shape, but at first she saw them only vaguely, lacking the sharp detail that feeling gives. Apparently, remembering the feelings was still too painful.

A few weeks later, Rachel and her children visited Aunt Margaret and she saw just how pinched and narrow her aunt was in dealing with children. Seeing her aunt with her own little girls made a part of Rachel see what she had been subject to—a part of her that had been not so much blind as constrained not to look. She began to grasp how complex and unattended her life was. There was no sudden and decisive epiphany, no "Aha!" that cures with dazzling insight. Instead, Rachel overcame her depression and became freer to choose her own way of life by a series of successive enrichments in perspective.

As we have seen, the midlife crisis does not depend solely upon stress or external life structure; one's own character and experience determine the ability to cope. But this explanation can lead to a negative implication: that the midlife crisis is a setback, confronting us with old psychic business. Psychic conflict may be a residue of the past, but it is wrong to think that at some point in life we either do or don't resolve our inner conflicts—the way we either pass or fail an examination. A more accurate (and optimistic) description is that the personality structure continues to evolve in a social context that changes with maturity.

6

The Empty Self

FREUDIAN conflict theory can explain many of the anxieties and depressions of midlife as the result of reawakened conflict between drives and the inner structures of culture. It cannot as well explain the despair of those who discover in middle age that the ambitions by which they have defined their basic patterns of self have not been realized. These people do not suffer so much from specific anxieties or acute depressions as from a profound inner emptiness.

What Freud did not fully appreciate is that we do not discharge instincts in a vacuum. Our most basic needs are expressed in relationship with other people. Moreover, these other people are more than convenient vehicles, "objects," for gratifying our sexual and aggressive needs; they and our relationships to them are essential to our very nature.

A series of *object relations* theorists, culminating with Heinz Kohut, developed the idea of the ego as the self, the real heart of the personality. Object relations theory focuses on the mental images we have of other people, built up from experience and expectation. These "inner objects" are often quite different from the real people of the external world. As adults, we react not only to the actual other, but also to an internal other. The residue of past relationships also leaves an internal image of the self in relation to others. When experience is painful, the true self is repressed and hidden behind a socially functioning conformist façade. Kohut's *psychology of the self* teaches that this true self may not even be consolidated and whole. The "empty self" erects an outer shell of conformity around a weak and immature ego. In contrast to Freudian psychology, this new perspective emphasizes inadequacy not conflict, deficiency not combat.

Inside all of us, a frightened child faces an unfriendly and menacing world. This timidity is seldom apparent, because we mask it in an attempt to live without conscious fears. But look around you, everywhere you will see contempt for and fear of weakness. Most of us are sufficiently self-confident for normal purposes, but deep within our being the frightened child remains.

This line of thinking is the link between Freudian conflict theory and the psychology of the self. According to both views the young child is helpless and absolutely dependent on parents. When they are absent or depriving, the child is lonely and terrified, and feels the bottom dropping out of the whole world. We are not used to thinking of the child's inner world as filled with terror. After all, babies are pretty resilient, aren't they? Yes, but one mechanism of this resiliency is repression. These primitive childhood fears are locked away in a dark corner of the mind, where they luxuriate like mushrooms in a cave. Every child is subject to morbid fears of abandonment, punishment, and emptiness. The more punitive or cold the parents are, the more they poison the child's passion for living and basic self-confidence.

This is not a pretty picture of childhood, and it is by no means the whole picture; but why else do children regularly wake up screaming during the period (from one to three) when they are sorting this all out? Growing up is a process of conquering some of these fears, repressing others. But, as we know, repression is not simply a matter of putting something away and forgetting about it. It requires constant effort to keep the lid on; we never really relax our guard. We spend our lives trying to feel secure in our own self-esteem, but weakness and dependency haunt us always. Here then is the bridge from the inner world of the child to the unconscious vulnerability of adults in midlife—helpless dependency as the fragile core of the self.

In addressing this problem, Heinz Kohut's brilliant writings, including *The Analysis of the Self* and *The Restoration of the Self*, have been vastly influential, and I will draw on them for many of the ideas here. There are, however, two problems that necessitate translation before Kohut's ideas can be applied to the midlife crisis. First, the central concept, "narcissism," is elusive, even misleading. Second, the particular subjects of his study were far more seriously disturbed than the many people who suffer a midlife crisis.

To most of us, narcissism means selfish preoccupation based on excessive admiration of oneself. It conjures up the myth of Narcissus, the Greek youth who pined away for love of his own reflection. In Freud's definition, "primary narcissism" is a stage of sexual development that precedes love for others. In early infancy, one's own body is the object of erotic interest. Later, the process of transferring sexual interest to others can miscarry, and the result is defensive withdrawal of libido from others and a reinvestment back onto the self. This is a kind of U-tube theory, with libido flowing either toward others or toward the self. The difference between Freud's meaning and Kohut's is the difference between self-love and self-doubt.

Healthy narcissism is a normal line of development throughout life. The goal is to transform childhood strivings for attention into mature ideals and ambitions. Healthy self-esteem—normal narcissism—is not reciprocally related to the capacity for loving others, as Freud thought. Common sense tells us that the person who genuinely loves self is more capable of loving others. Ideas to the contrary come from mistaking meticulous preoccupation with one's appearance as evidence of self-love. Most people strain for glimpses of themselves in the mirror, not to admire themselves, but to see if they are okay.

In the psychology of the self, "narcissistic" means inner emptiness and hunger for attention and praise, not selfishness (at least not in its ordinary perjorative sense). By "narcissism" Kohut means fragile self-esteem resulting in a preoccupation with how one is doing and how well one is regarded by others. More than mere egocentricity, this means chasing the illusion of specialness in order to compensate for inner feelings of inadequacy. The preoccupation with fantasies of success and the excessive need to be loved and admired comes not from arrogance, but from emptiness. Something vital is missing. In moments of despair there may be a feeling of loneliness, a feeling of being nothing, confusion, and a sense of being uncared for. This inner emptiness is rarely conscious, fortunately, for it is hard to bear.

The pathological narcissism Kohut describes *is* pathological; the people he treats *are* disturbed; but the narcissistic struggle he describes is too widespread to be an aberration. The most inadequate solutions may be the easiest to observe, but the basic problem is ubiquitous.

The Development of the Self

To understand how the self develops and how this development can miscarry, we need to understand something about the psychological birth of the human infant. Physiologically this tiny creature is already remarkably complex, but psychologically it is not yet a person. The baby depends for physical survival on the care of parents; the baby's psychological birth depends upon them as well, and the outcome is determined in large part by the nature of that care.

To the very young child, parents are not quite separate individuals; they are, in Kohut's terms, "self-objects," people experienced as parts of the self. As a self-object, the mother transmits her calmness and love by touch, tone of voice, and gentle words, as though they were the child's own feelings. When she whispers, "Mommy loves you," the baby learns that he or she is (a) a person and (b) lovable. Steady, loving parental validation nourishes a lifelong sense of security.

In self psychology, two qualities of parenting are considered essential for the establishment of a secure and cohesive self. The first is *empathy*—understanding plus acceptance. A small child requires admiring acceptance of his or her healthy self-assertiveness in order to develop a firm sense of worth. Attentive parents convey a deep understanding of how their children feel. Their implicit "I see how you feel" helps confirm the validity and acceptability of the child's inner experience. (By the way, empathy can be given most freely by those people capable of recognizing their children's feelings without actually having to feel them [sympathy] or being compelled to let the children act on the basis of their feelings.)

The parents must also offer a model for *identification*. The little child who can believe "My father (or mother) is terrific and I am part of him (or her)" has a firm base of self-esteem. In the best of circumstances, the child, already basically secure in his or her self, draws additional strength from identifying with the apparently infinite power and strength of the parents. But if parents fail to offer sufficient praise and reassurance, children can compensate by sharing in the parents' obvious competence. If a child were able to verbalize this experience, he or she might say, "Maybe Mommy didn't tell me that I am a wonderful child, but I am going to grow up to be just as strong and smart as she is."

Long before the baby achieves self-consciousness, the parents invest it with their expectations and aspirations. From day one, they relate to the baby as both an actual and a potential self. Once the child becomes a self, a separate and cohesive entity, the process of discovering what kind of self begins. Invention is part of the process too, as the child's own creative self-definition is actively shaped and molded by the parents' responses.

Normally, a growing child explores his or her relationship to the world, protected from harm by watchful parents and confirmed as a worthwhile person by their loving attention. When a toddler proudly waddles across the room, the parents greet the achievement with hugs and words of praise. The child experiences the enthusiastic response as acceptance, not only of walking, but also of the developing self.

However, more often than not, flesh-and-blood parents mix praise with rejection. Ten minutes after a toddler is rewarded for walking across the room, he or she may be scolded harshly for reaching out to touch a shiny object—mommy's crystal bowl. Selective acceptance on the part of the parents is partly deliberate, partly inadvertent. Parents want to encourage certain potentials in their children, but they ignore some forms of self-expression, while actively discouraging others. In this way parents transmit the values of culture as well as their own view of what children should do and be. This is a natural and constructive process of education. How it is done, though, makes a great deal of difference. Remember that the child takes acceptance or rejection not only as judgment of particular activities but also as acceptance or rejection of self.

Loving caretakers allow their children to establish and then slowly dissolve dependent relationships. In this way, parental admiration and inspiration become part of the child's inner resources. Minor or sporadic failures of empathy are not destructive; but if a mother continues to be disinterested or rejecting, the child will feel empty and worthless. Or, as is more usual, if she responds only to a fragment of the child's developing self—putting emphasis on, say, neatness or achievement— the child will feel worthwhile only about this aspect of the total self. Intuitively aware of this, the good parent communicates understanding first and then responds with selective criticism. Haim Ginott, who popularized this principle in *Between Parent and Child*, advised parents to discipline or control their children only after acknowledging the child's feelings. An example of this two-step process is, "I understand, you feel like making a pretty picture on the wall . . . but walls are not for drawing on."

The little child (and the insecure adult) needs this kind of love and acceptance far more than any other form of teaching or shaping. Loving confirmation is the prerequisite to a stable and secure self. Later, after a sturdy foundation is laid, there is plenty of time for guidance and selective molding. The ideal is acceptance first, followed by healthy frustration.

In our child-centered culture, some parents are *too* tolerant. Confusing acceptance with indulgence, they set few limits, whether material or emotional. When every wish is gratified, every whim catered to, the child is ill-equipped for the compromises necessary to get along in the "real world." What's worse, the child does not even have the compensation of a secure self. There is a price tag for overindulgence. The doting parent usually disregards or opposes the child's growing independence and autonomy. Only that part of the self—dependence—that is in tune with the parent's need is nurtured.

Other parents put their own needs ahead of the needs of their children and as a result are emotionally unavailable. Their behavior is not generally deliberate. It's based on their own insecurity, emotional shallowness, or depression. Occasional insensitivity to a child's needs and feelings may cause no permanent harm, but when it is chronic and pervasive, the outcome is an insecure and feeble self. Consider the following scenario: A little girl comes home from nursery school, eager to show her mother a new finger painting. The mother responds by asking, "What is it?" and then proceeds to demonstrate how she would have done it better. As the little girl listens, her glow of pride fades; she becomes convinced that what she thought was a good job wasn't so good after all, and her image of herself shrinks in the process.

Here we have a commonplace exchange in which the parent's reflected appraisal affects the child's evolving sense of self. The basic self, its relative cohesion and strength, is formed in such interactions. Things can go wrong from the start. When they do, analysts tend to blame the parents, especially the mother. This is a product of linear thinking, according to which the world is made up of victims and victimizers, and most of us identify with the victims. The result of this collusion reinforces the natural tendency to attribute problems to external sources.

From the outset, the formative parent-child interactions are circular. A baby's reaction to a mother's lack of responsiveness is withdrawal, which in turn pushes the mother farther away. Thereafter baby and mother continue to influence each other in a series of moves and countermoves—a dance whose beginning is less relevant than its perpetuation. Nor, to set the record straight, does the process necessarily begin with the mother. Natural variations in a baby's constitution and temperament affect the mother's response almost from the moment of birth. Some babies are so demanding that their mothers feel beleaguered beyond endurance. Such babies will be made to feel that their demands are excessive—and that they, themselves, are bad by nature. Some babies are so placid that they don't elicit sufficient attention to feel loved and admired. To further complicate matters, many babies are born into households already shaped by the parents' previous experience with other children. If the firstborn was so demanding that the mother was left exhausted and emotionally depleted, the second infant may not get much attention, especially if he or she is a quiet baby.

In addition to being circular, the mother-child interaction— like all significant human relationships—is also triangular. A woman's response to her child is determined not only by her personality and the infant's disposition, but also by her relationship with her husband. If she feels nourished in a loving adult relationship, the mother can respond empathically to the emotional needs of her children. But if there is no sustaining adult relationship, she may satisfy her own needs through her children, to the detriment of their self-development.

Fathers of course are important too, not only indirectly

through their relationships to mothers, but also in their direct contact with children. In harmonious families fathers respond empathically to their children, forming a cohesive parental bond and doubling the children's positive experience. In families where the mother is harshly critical or unresponsive, fathers have an extra responsibility to provide affirmation and encouragement. This, unfortunately, seldom happens. Despite recent changes in masculine image toward a softer, more whole man, our culture continues to expect very little from fathers. We still applaud the few fathers who lend a hand in caring for their children and tend to tolerate those who don't.

The Empty Self

If the childhood need to be admired and confirmed is frustrated, it is intensified into a lasting craving. The child grows to adulthood with a piece close to the heart left behind. These people look like grown-ups, but the tenuous quality of their selfhood leaves them with childlike dependency on others for reassurance and praise. Exhibitionism is not sublimated, it is repressed. The child who hungered in vain for praise becomes an adult who alternately suppresses the craving for attention, then lets it break through in an all-or-nothing form in the presence of anyone who seems safe and receptive. "Look at me," cries the little child. "Look at what I've done," says the adult. Maybe by becoming the best parent ever, the perfect worker, the best-dressed person in the office, smarter, better-looking, stronger—more and more, better and better—maybe then the adult will feel secure, worthwhile, and lovable.

The empty self relates to others as means to ends rather than as ends in themselves. These narcissistic people may seek out admiration and acceptance, but they really want reassurance, not human company. If selfishness means unconcern with others, these people are just the opposite. They are obsessed with the opinion of others and have an inordinate need to be loved and admired. Status seekers are careful to wear the correct clothes, to be seen in the right places with the right people. These are the people who measure their worth by conspicuous consumption and change their habits to keep up with what is in style. They may be too busy to enjoy their possessions; still, they collect them as marks of status. Fame seekers want approval from the eyes of a larger public; it is a grander, but more distanced acclaim that they crave. And narcissism is easily recognized in the preoccupation with uniqueness of many professional performers.

Many of us, however, have better social covers for the same yearnings. Some may ward off low self-esteem with defensive self-inflation, but most show their self-doubt more openly. We feign modesty, while working hard and dreaming of grand success; we cultivate reputations for loyalty, while drawing confidence from the reflected glory of those we lean on; we seek "feedback," but are shaken badly by criticism and disappointment.

Phil was on the managerial fast track of a large corporation, until, at the age of forty-two, he was "laterally promoted" to a district manager's position, which meant he had gone as far as he could with the company. When he first consulted me, "for career counseling," he was too preoccupied with finding a new job to feel the depression that set in later. At first his conversation was frantically upbeat: "A lot of guys get upset by these things, but I haven't got time for that; I've got to redo my résumé, make some calls, and get the word out that I'm available." And he was full of denial that he felt hurt or rejected: "I don't view this as a valid statement of my value to the organization. The politics in the home office are byzantine. Those people wouldn't know talent if it hit them over the head.

Moving me to the midwest office is a stupid mistake." Here was the tough corporate executive fighting back. But when Phil ran out of steam a couple of weeks later, depression set in.

The company, he now felt, was right. "I don't have what it takes to get to the top. . . . I guess I never did." For a time he was extremely unhappy, but in a vague sort of way. He began to think of his problems as part of the inevitable process of entering middle age. That gave him a different perspective —not that he was a failure but that growing up means giving up grandiose dreams—and that was easier to live with.

He tried to tell himself that fame and fortune weren't essential to a happy life. He even quoted an expert author to that effect. But Phil made the same mistake a lot of people do: confusing what should be with what is. Maybe people *shouldn't* want or need external success to make them feel worthwhile. Unfortunately, many people *do*, and Phil was one of them.

The depression returned, only now it was worse. Phil felt a deep sense of personal inadequacy; it had always been there, but he had been too busy with the office wars to notice. Phil came from a midwestern farm family; they had few luxuries, and when the weather was cruel, hardly enough to feed and clothe them all. It was this poverty, Phil thought, that drove him toward material success.

In our sessions, a portrait of his parents emerged. Phil's mother was stern and strong. She worked hard, and he admired her. Without her, Phil knew, the farm would have failed. But she was also austere and distant. A strong fundamentalist upbringing had left her with the conviction that life is serious business. She had little time for relaxation or tenderness.

Still, Phil's mother was never deliberately cruel, and from time to time she gave him the praise and attention for which he longed. Because she was inconsistent, he kept hoping; because he kept hoping, he left himself wide open to repeated hurts. Gradually, however, he turned away and erected an elaborate system of defenses to protect himself. Outwardly, he grew tough; but no system of defenses could totally protect him. That would have taken a lead shield.

The nurturing function, usually provided by mothers in our culture, is the main chance we have to grow up secure and proud. But most children get a second chance. Often, a child who is disappointed by a lack of maternal responsiveness turns to the father. Phil wasn't lucky there either.

He hardly spoke of his father in the first weeks of treatment. When I called this to his attention, he said, "My father was a weakling and a drunkard." Phil told me, with obvious suffering, of the countless times his father came home drunk, and how his mother's anger turned to despair. Whether this pitiless image was formed solely by the little boy's judgment or whether it was picked up from an angry wife's distortion is beside the point. In either case, Phil grew up with a paternal model that gave him little comfort. Consciously, he took pains never to be like his father. Secretly, he feared that he was cast in the same mold. The result was a guilty self-denial of the pleasures of life, which is often taken as a sign of unconscious fear of punishment. But Phil wasn't afraid of his drives; he just didn't want to be like his father. His real fear was that he already was. His depression was brought on not by losing something, but by finding himself inadequate.

Phil's successful treatment was based on insight. His first step was to get a good grasp on what was happening to him in the present. He *had* suffered a sharp setback to his career; it was a loss to be mourned, and a blow to be healed.

The mourning had already begun. It started when Phil stopped denying that the "lateral promotion" was a serious disappointment. Overcoming a loss requires facing and feeling the fact of the loss; for Phil this meant overcoming his tendency to "cheer up and look on the bright side." Repairing the blow to his self-image was a little more complicated. This, too, began with accepting the reality of what had happened. Phil's failure to be promoted *was* a comment on himself. What Phil had to understand was why success had become so critical to his self-esteem.

Gradually, the insecurity underlying Phil's ambition began to emerge. Beneath the bravado, the fragile sense of himself; and beneath that, the longings for love and admiration. This is one time when a therapist can be very helpful. When repression lifts, that which was repressed is likely to be too painful to tolerate and may be pushed away. Phil was inclined to be very critical of his feelings of inadequacy and his yearning for approval. (His parents' harsh voices still spoke inside him.) What he needed was not so much an interpretation of his unconscious anxieties, but empathy, humanizing with acceptance the feelings he was ashamed of.

For Phil, the first kind of understanding (or insight) was cognitive; he learned that his parents' response to him was more an indication of what sort of people they were than a measure of his true self. The second kind of understanding was emotional; he repeated with me his need for a mirror of his healthy self-pride. When he bragged of his worth, I didn't "interpret" the insecurity beneath it; I reflected his ambition with statements like "Yes, wouldn't it be wonderful to be on top of the heap" and "You've longed to be that powerful and that strong since you were a kid."

As he learned to believe in himself, Phil no longer needed my sustaining empathy. By accepting his ambitions *and* his limits, he was able to function with a greater range of alternatives, albeit with a conscious awareness of realistic limitations.

Phil's story can stand for many of us.

The Traumas of Midlife

What is there about middle age so likely to expose the inner emptiness of an insecure self? Or, put another way, what is there about midlife that is so likely to cause narcissistic injury? To answer this, let's review some of the stresses of midlife described earlier: coming to terms with the limits of success, giving up dependency relationships at home and at work, signs of physical aging, contemplation of time running out. Here are the same dilemmas that have been said to *cause* the midlife crisis. The familiar psychological challenges of middle age don't cause despair, but they are well-suited to provoke it in those with fragile inner selves.

Like Phil, confusing courage with fearlessness, we tell ourselves, "I'm tough," and in the process become accomplished liars—to the world and to ourselves. We all need illusions, but some of us invest so much in our dreams that we don't have enough left over for reality. If this tendency characterizes everyone to a certain extent, where do we cross the line into a crisis in midlife?

Certain individuals cannot face their fears of helpless dependency. In their protective self-inflation they manufacture illusions of strength. Some protect their self-esteem by restricting their experience, avoiding tests of life that they might fail. Chastened by old hurts, they neglect friendship. Afraid of failure, they do not seek out professional challenges. These people glorify themselves in fantasy instead of fashioning a creative relationship to work and to other people; they cannot risk their self-esteem enough to plunge into full participation in life. In midlife they find it harder to deceive themselves.

Other people work hard to make their fantasies come true, chasing unrealistic goals. These people actually try to build a glorified world and may attempt creative work. But their efforts are often driven by a joyless compulsion that is hard to distinguish from a clinical obsession. These people eventually exhaust themselves in self-preoccupation. The more we inflate ourselves, the more vulnerable we are to disillusion. At middle age, some people who cannot say, "I am everything," begin to say, "I am nothing."

American men and women in the 1980s have to cope with rapid social changes that further undermine the outer supports to self-esteem. We are turning forty in a very different world from the one in which our expectations were formed. Our parents and grandparents worked hard, but their expectations were different. For them, personal satisfaction from work was less of a consideration; they were too busy providing for their families to consider their own fulfillment. Today's troublesome economy means that most of us will work harder in our forties, but have less—less for ourselves and less to give our children. Many of us can't help interpreting economic insecurity as evidence of personal failure.

To the self-doubting, shifting sex roles suggest more than that the rules are changing; they think they must have been wrong in their assumptions. Women of the eighties have to deal with the effects of new roles on old fears. Despite dramatic changes in their exterior lives, women's inner anxieties may not differ significantly from those of their mothers. The primary anxiety for many women is fear of abandonment, rejection, and loss of love. A classic example is the woman who achieves great career success, but feels shattered when a love relationship breaks up.

Today's men are also facing a new age with old anxieties. The primordial male fear is tied to performance and success. Economic realities make it harder to achieve success, and the demands of liberated women for fuller satisfaction have increased male anxieties about sexual performance. The new cultural norm calls on men to be softer and less aggressive, but consciously held gender stereotypes have proven easier to change than unconscious definitions of the self. Disappointments in work and loss of mastery in the personal sphere still stir deep feelings of inadequacy.

Many men of our generation were weaned on the notion that power is gained in the marketplace. Relationships outside of business were secondary and therefore often shallow or exploitive. One version of this model is the ebullient, indefatigable achiever, who gets what he wants by hard work and fast talking. Another version is the strong silent type, will-driven and self-sufficient. In either case, aggressiveness and independence are likely to organize the relationships of these men. Their relentless need to validate their selves is especially sad because it is frequently so self-defeating. By trying to shore up flagging self-esteem through outward success, these men often neglect their families—where they *could* find love and confirmation.

In a culture that conveys its highest prizes for competitive dominance, women as well as men seek rank and status as a defense against feelings of inadequacy. Despite this, however, we remain most vulnerable to rejection from the families we sometimes take for granted. The mortification comes from reexposure to the narcissistic injuries of childhood, and the hurt goes to the heart of the self.

Walter and Gail, a married couple, provide an example. They came for marital therapy shortly after he discovered that she was having an affair. While looking through her purse for the car keys, he found a letter that made everything clear. "I never suspected anything," he said, "never, never . . ." and then broke off in tears.

During the next several weeks, Walter and Gail went through a fairly standard sequence of events for couples in this predicament. His initial shock and hurt turned to anger—after all, it feels psychologically safer to be angry than to be vulnerable. He threatened to divorce Gail and take the children. He even consulted a lawyer who told him that he would have a good chance to win custody if he acted quickly.

After a time, though, Walter realized that he loved his wife and didn't want to divorce her. "Maybe I made some mistakes too," he said; and he went on to acknowledge that he had taken Gail for granted in the early years of the marriage. This was enough of an opening for his wife to risk airing some of her complaints. With therapeutic support she began to describe her feelings of neglect while Walter was investing so much energy in his career. Now that a constructive problem-solving atmosphere was established, the couple was able to take steps to improve their relationship. Fortunately the bond they had was strong enough to withstand a severe shock; now they could build a marriage with enough give-and-take to keep them both satisfied. Or so it seemed.

What made this case different from so many others was that Walter could not seem to get over what had happened. Normally it takes time to get over such a hurt—not exactly to forget, but to get over it. In a case like this, it might take six months to a year for the process to run its course. But Walter couldn't forget.

Weeks would go by when he wouldn't bring up the affair, but then he would become moody and dejected, a surefire sign that he was reliving the injury to his pride and self-esteem. Talking about it—the penicillin of psychotherapy—didn't help either. Here the formula "depression = loss" didn't work. Careful attention to Walter's comments made it clear that his major reaction to the infidelity was as a reflection of his own inadequacy. He experienced his love rejected not primarily as a loss, but as confirmation of his lifelong fear that he was not lovable. The affair, like other difficulties in real life, could be accepted, met, and coped with *except* that it touched a raw nerve ending in Walter's core self-esteem.

Once he realized that his wife was not responsible for what he felt—her affair was the irritant, but the real wound was much deeper—Walter asked to be seen in individual therapy. My job then was to avoid "interpretations" that might feel more like criticism than enlightenment. His job was to overcome a lifetime of practiced impression management and to admit feelings of wanting to be special and fears that he wasn't. With the support of therapy over many weeks, Walter allowed his strivings full expression. In the process, my acceptance offered him a model that he was gradually able to internalize.

Narcissistic injury can follow success as well as failure. Though this may be hard to understand, there are many people for whom no amount of adult achievement can resolve unfulfilled childhood needs. To make it worse, no matter how successful these people are, life seems to hold more failure than success.

From her first day on the sales force of a prestigious company, Sally dreamed of winning the annual sales award, and she worked hard to make the dream a reality. Eighteen months later, Sally was elated to learn that she had won the top sales prize in her district office. But after a few days, the elation gave way to depression.

There are two conventional explanations for Sally's depression: she was threatened by the consequences of an oedipal victory, or she had a "fear of success," as it is called these days. The first explanation is often useful, but did not apply here. Sally felt no remorse at having defeated a powerful rival, no guilt at attaining something forbidden. But as soon as she won the prize for her district, she became aware that it wasn't the *grand* prize—the national award—and at some level she realized that no matter what the prize, it wouldn't be enough. Despite her success, she was nagged by a secret fear that she was a fraud and would be exposed.

The second explanation, "fear of success," is heavily freighted with sexist assumptions. Although Freud spoke of both men and women who are "wrecked by success," this theory is most often applied to women. Can a woman really want success? Wasn't Sally's career obviously some kind of compensation for her failure to marry young? Doesn't achievement threaten a woman like Sally's undeniable need to be "feminine"? The answers to these questions are yes, no, and no, respectively.

Sally's history revealed a disappointing relationship with her mother. Often depressed, Sally's mother had little time for her youngest daughter, and so Sally sought approval from her hard-driving father by adopting his ideals: success, achievement, and power. The father's approval, though given, was conditional. Her achievements, as he often reminded Sally, were "good but not great." The father was himself a narcissistic personality, and his children were only agents of his ambition. When they were little, he took pride in showing them off; as they grew older, he tried to enlist them as surrogates for his own accomplishment. The older children, who grew up before their mother gave way to depression, managed to resist his influence. Sally, to the extent that her mother was emotionally unavailable, turned to her father.

Unfortunately, she also adopted his fallacious definition of power. Real power is the ability to act effectively; it comes from the things that a person naturally does well and then works hard to improve. But Sally, like her father, confused power with manipulating people to win their admiration.

What kept her going? And what was so decisive about the effect of winning the sales award? What kept her going was just enough paternal praise to sustain her fragile self. In addition, she learned how to protect herself by not exposing her need for approval. So, alternating between defensiveness and partial successes, she managed to get by. The sales award was symbolically so important that it reawakened hidden childhood needs for loving admiration. Winning it allowed a repressed exhibitionistic self to emerge. Suddenly, she was no longer a powerful woman, but a girlish self who yearned in vain for confirmation from both parents.

The sad truth is that no matter how many awards we win, love will not be among them. Sally learned that the search for self-esteem through accomplishment is chimerical—but only after having achieved a modicum of success. Then she discovered that she could give meaning to her life simply through living it fully.

Transforming the Dreamer

The spreading waistline and lost zip of midlife are as painful to some people as were the acne and growth spurts of adolescence. These changes are usually thought threatening because they detract from youthful ideals of physical beauty. This is certainly true, but changes in the body are more or less disturbing depending upon the firmness of the self—not only the pride of intrinsic self-worth, but also the sureness that comes from a sense of being a cohesive self that endures change.

Today's women are twice cursed; caught between conflicting values of what it means to be female, they are likely to suffer confusion at midlife. No matter what they have learned as liberated adults, today's forty-year-old women were taught as children that their power comes mainly from youthful allure and that at a certain age they will begin to lose it. Now, the narcissistic blow is compounded by shame over still needing to feel beautiful.

For men it is supposed to be different. A man has many pathways to power in our culture, especially if he retains his health and enthusiasm. Aren't we far more likely to accept an older man with a younger woman than the reverse? But men in their forties with fragile selves are especially threatened by outward signs of change, and the greatest fear of all—one's own mortality—preys most heavily on the grown-up child who has always feared disintegration of the self.

The narcissistic injuries, which are the *agents provocateurs* of the midlife crisis, hardly need further elaboration at this point. Less obvious but equally significant are the setbacks caused by disappointments in figures of identification. Mentor relationships, so important to young adults, are lost in midlife. Whether we become disillusioned with our mentors or simply outgrow them, by midlife we are on our own. Still we are not without models.

It may not happen at twenty-one, but by forty our relationship with our parents is no longer that of a child to an adult. If we are lucky it becomes adult to adult; if not, the roles of adult and child may reverse. In either case, it seems that we no longer take our parents as ideals. In fact, we may have outgrown them. A middle-aged woman looks in the mirror and sees her mother's expression; a man hears himself making the same stupid puns his father did. Both feel that they have been hiding from the truth: they were always destined to grow up like their parents, with all their parents' flaws. In youth, we conceal our heritage, but in maturity it breaks through.

Taking care of sick parents casts one in a role of strength, but forecasts a future of decline. "My mother always turned to me for strength," a woman patient told me, "and that made me feel really adult. If I am my mother's mother then I will never be a child again. At first the switch in roles gave me a tremendous feeling of confidence, but over the years taking care of her wore me out. And, worse, I begin to see her depression in me. True, I was still functioning at a high level, but I realized that my periodic gloominess would someday make me just like her. Here I am at the peak of my power, but doomed to end up like my mother."

A parallel process may occur with our own offspring. When we catch ourselves living out our parents' failings in our relations with our children, the hurt to our self-image is magnified by the realization of what we are doing to theirs. Commonplace failings, like getting a speeding ticket, are more self-diminishing when our kids are witness to our ineptitude. We see our shortcomings reflected in the disillusioned eyes of our children, and our narcissism suffers keenly. These little episodes may bring back scenes from our own childhood—the time our mother got drunk or father lost a job—indelibly embedded both in our memories and, unconsciously, as gaps in our self-esteem.

The inevitable recognition of limits and finitude topple the myths of omnipotence and grandiosity by which people with weak and empty selves sustain themselves through youth into midlife. Doesn't this explanation simply reinforce the prevalent notion that adjustment to maturity means giving up grandiose goals? Scale down your dreams, accept who you are, and take life for what it is?

Unfortunately this advice has limited usefulness in the face of psychic reality. Guiding dreams cannot be changed at will, like a suit of clothes. They may be unrealistically grand, but denying them does not diminish their hold on the imagination. Dreams persist until the dreamer is transformed; then they are not given up—they just lose their meaning and their power.

For the dream of grand achievement to lose its hypnotic grip, the dreamer must gradually internalize a sense of worth. This does not come from a conscious decision to give up dreams of self-aggrandizement, but from accepting and enriching relationships with other people. Healing relations are possible in midlife, but they may not come easily—especially if we cling to the idea that we are autonomous selves.

The myth of the separate self pervades our view of normal adulthood. Growing up means giving up the past, part of which is believed to be a person's ties to the family. Most people acknowledge the value of human relationships, but see them as something a person chooses. The mature man, according to the usual view, is a separate being, free from the automatic entanglements of family. He is not alone, though, because he *chooses* to be with people—what is usually called "attachment." Women don't have to cultivate attachment—it is drilled into them from an early age. The seasons of a man's life may be ordered by separation, but the theme of a woman's life is attachment. True, men and women differ: women are brought up to value affectionate regard for and devotion to others, while most men must cultivate it. But, however they may differ, both sexes are equally anchored in a network of human relations, from which they cannot be separate.

The concept of a separate self is a useful adolescent notion. It teaches youngsters to be responsible, to learn to think for themselves, and to strive not to compromise their beliefs. For teenagers, separation is the standard avenue of growth. But this process can be very difficult for young people in conflict about their need for dependency. Needing the family, but used to rebuff, dependency becomes a sign of weakness. Thus, the normal tendency to define a self divorced from the family is exaggerated in insecure people. Ironically, the motivating desire for love and admiration drives them *away* from the one source most likely to provide it.

The self is not a separate entity, a moveable monad that can be separated from the family if one chooses. Like all creatures of nature, we are inextricably embedded in a social context, the center and heart of which is the family. Realizing this does not do away with hard choices, but it puts them in a new perspective, which has far-reaching implications for resolving the crises of midlife.

7

The Power of Families

HUMAN beings are social beings. From the moment of birth we seek not simply tension-reduction but relatedness; loving human bonds are what sustain us. When we think of the self in isolation, it is an artificial abstraction, reinforced by defensive flight from the hurts and disappointments to which our natural dependence exposes us. If only we could banish the anxiety of being connected, of needing and being needed by other people, surely then we would be free. But there is a paradox. As long as we refuse to acknowledge our connection to others, we can never be fully reconciled to ourselves. Icarus sought to be free, but he could not be free of his earthbound nature, and so in the end he fell. We do need other people, and we are part of them. This is the larger truth about human nature: each of us is part of a system greater than ourselves.

The most powerful system is, of course, the family. The family is more than a collection of separate individuals; it is an organic whole whose parts function together in a way that transcends their separate characteristics. This concept of systems is useful but slippery. With a little effort it is possible to grasp it in dry abstractions, but when you try to apply it to yourself, it often slips away.

Trained observers have learned to see the unity of families. A man and a woman argue until their child begins to cry. They break off the argument to comfort the child. The woman, still angry, leaves the house. The man is left to look after the child. The longer his wife is gone, the more resentful he becomes. When she returns the couple begins to argue again—until the child cries. In this sequence, we can see an elaborate dance with each move choreographed by the one preceding it and shaping the one that follows.

A similar situation exists in the natural world. Puzzling events in nature can sometimes be understood only after the system in which they are embedded is recognized. Some years ago, wildlife biologists in Canada noticed that the rabbit population rose and fell in cycles of three years. Why this happened and why the cycle took exactly three years remained a mystery. The scientists checked for disease, drought, and migration; still they found nothing to explain the strange cyclical pattern. Finally the mystery was solved when the scientists discovered that the population of foxes showed a complementary rise and fall. In the first year of the cycle, rabbits were abundant. In the second year, the foxes, who prey on the rabbits, had more than enought to eat, and so they became plentiful. When the foxes were numerous, the rabbit population declined sharply. Then in the following year, with their natural source of food in short supply, many foxes starved, making it possible once again for the rabbits to multiply like rabbits.

Even with college educations, it is unlikely that foxes and rabbits would recognize themselves as part of a single system. We humans also experience ourselves as individuals, and it usually takes an outsider to see members of a system interacting as a structured whole. Certainly we recognize that we affect others and they affect us. Still, we continue to think of ourselves as separate units interacting with other units.

When we do consider our connection with our families, it is often in terms of the constraints and demands they place on us. This is especially noticeable when we deviate from usual patterns or expectations. If, for example, a husband and father considers taking a job in a different city, his family may resist the change. In some families, even minor changes in established ritual are occasions for protest. Coming home from work ten minutes later than usual can provoke anxious concern or angry criticism. Normally, this regulating process in the family system operates automatically and outside of awareness. Motivations can remain obscure. A man may turn on the television set to watch the news, unaware that he does so to sidestep conversation with his wife. A woman may become overweight without realizing that she does so partly to circumvent her husband's jealousy of other men. Unless we undertake some major change, we rarely see our behavior as part of a systemic, recurring cycle. A husband thinks he withdraws because his wife nags; she thinks that she nags only because he withdraws. They do not realize that they are partners in the same ballet.

The idea of families as systems is of special interest to family therapists and anyone who treats troubled families. Once the family is understood as structured by an invisible set of functional demands, it becomes possible to decipher—and resolve —problems that are otherwise as perplexing as the rabbit/fox mystery.

Therapists first encountered the family system as a powerful adversary. Over and again they were defeated by the family's influence over their individual patients. Families, they discovered, act like organisms; the more fragile they are, the more they resist change. Most families will do anything to avoid disrupting their equilibrium, even if it means scapegoating their children or sacrificing a parent's sanity to maintain the family's stability. And so the concept of the family as a system evolved, and along with it the theory that change in *one* person changes the whole system. This deceptively simple statement has more profound consequences than saying people are "influenced by their interactions."

Systems in Formation: Accommodation and Boundaries

Family systems begin with the union of two separate personalities. When we were young, we thought this beginning was an ending, the "happy ending" we read about in books and saw in the movies. Back then, the search for love was the drama of our lives. Finding someone was supposed to be the hard part. Once we found someone to love, we expected to marry and "live happily ever after."

Most people *are* happy when they get married; that's why they get married. Courtship is deliciously romantic, and when we are in love, life is rich and beautiful. New couples are ripe with possibility; everything seems possible. Over time they become progressively structured as a system, organized by the demands of living together and raising a family. At first, the patterns they establish to form a stable and coherent couple are free to vary; later they may become entrenched.

Young couples in love often have unrealistic ideas about marriage. The idealized fiction that normal family life is problem-free creates expectations that are hard to live up to. Measured against our blissful daydreams, the reality of everyday difficulties may seem cruelly unfair. We may think we're being reasonable, but many of us are secretly (and some not so secretly) outraged when our spouses don't automatically fulfill our expectations. Some of us simply fantasize that our problems would go away if only our partners would change. In fact, what distinguishes a good marriage from a bad one is not the absence of problems, but a well-functioning structure for dealing with them. One of the cornerstones of this structure is *accommodation.*

Many of us who were born in the forties and fifties grew up with the example of traditional roles for men and women. These sex-role stereotypes allowed our parents to achieve complementarity, but perhaps at the expense of truly rounded functioning for each spouse. A traditional middle-class woman was not expected to speak up, earn a living, or change a flat tire. In exchange, however, she may have had to downplay her intelligence, give up her vocation, and live in the shadow of her husband. Her counterpart, the traditional husband, was allowed to make the major decisions, avoided the drudgery of housework, and may have expected to be waited on hand and foot. The price for these "masculine" prerogatives was hiding his feelings, sole financial responsibility for the family, and little contact with his children.

Today, these rigid patterns are breaking down. Those of us who married in the sixties or late fifties may have started out these relationships in a traditional way; now as couples we are becoming more symmetrical. New options are thus created for each individual, but there are new strains as we must repeat and refine the process of accommodation we thought was behind us.

In every relationship, each partner expects to follow familiar forms. Each tries to duplicate the family he or she grew up in and pressures the partner to conform. Inevitably, each will have some areas where it is hard to be flexible. She may be willing to move across the country (her mother willingly followed where her father's career led), but finds it virtually impossible to wake up before 8 A.M. He may find it easy to cook supper (his father often cooked breakfast on Sunday), but be unwilling to eat meatless meals.

Both partners come to marriage with a different set of experiences and expectations. They may have talked over some of these issues when they were courting—whether or not to have children, where they will live, and so forth—but some things seem too trivial to discuss—what kind of food to buy, who will take out the garbage. Other matters, which each takes for granted as "the right way to do things," can lead to painful collisions. A man may assume that once they are married the couple will have sex every day; his wife may expect to continue the pattern established during courtship of having sex only on the weekends. He expects that they will commute to and from work together; she expects to continue having a drink with her friends after work.

Some of these differences are worked out easily. Accommodation works best when each partner has a sense of giving in order to get. "Sure, I'll do this for you (because I am confident that you will do things for me in return)." Some things, however, prove harder to negotiate. He's upset that she still wants to hang around with her friends after work; she feels smothered by his demands for exclusivity. The most painful struggles often revolve around *boundaries,* those invisible membranes that surround individuals and groups, regulating the amount of contact they have with others.

Firm boundaries keep people separate and enhance their independence and autonomy; permeable boundaries allow more contact, affection, and support. During courtship, most couples establish an extremely diffuse boundary between them:

they want to be together, to share each other's thoughts and feelings, and to cling to each other as much as possible. When infatuation fades, things change.

Among the elaborate set of expectations we all bring to marriage are assumptions about boundaries, that is, about "the right amount" of separateness and togetherness. We are most comfortable with the degree of proximity we grew up with. If our parents did everything together, we will expect to do the same; if our parents were independent, we will try to duplicate this relationship in our own marriages. It's hard not to take your own built-in preference for emotional closeness or distance as *the* standard. Those on the separateness end of the spectrum think of themselves as "self-reliant" and "independent," in contrast to others who are "dependent," "clinging," or even "smothering." People who are togetherness-oriented are likely to think of themselves as "close," "loving," and "affectionate," as opposed to others who are "distant," "cold," "aloof." It's tough when these "others" live at the same mailing address.

Conflicts over togetherness and separateness are notoriously hard to resolve, because they go to the core of personality. In the process of regulating distance/closeness, new couples oscillate between a point of equilibrium. This is how they establish the boundary in their relationship. Some couples cannot tolerate separateness, while others are unable to unite. When the boundary between the spouses is highly permeable, the couple exists primarily as a pair, which gradually erodes their separate personalities. These couples are likely to come from what family therapist Salvador Minuchin calls "enmeshed" families, tightly interlocked systems whose members are intensely preoccupied with each other.

At the other end of the continuum are "disengaged" couples, family universes in which the members revolve around each other in separate orbits, synchronized but rarely touching. Are enmeshment and disengagement in the person or in the system? Actually, a little of both.

Some people find intimacy difficult and therefore are anxious if they are too close for too long. These people never learned to trust others or give themselves freely in relationships. They have trouble relating to others; anxiety holds them back. During courtship, when anxiety is low, their need for emotional distance may not be apparent. Later on, when inevitable conflict comes into the marriage, the distancing pattern surfaces like an iceberg in the fog.

Deep-seated anxiety limits the appetite for intimacy in these people, predisposing them to keep their distance. At the same time attachments elsewhere—in the larger system—may exert their pull. The consequences need not be negative. For example, a commuter marriage, in which the partners are only together on weekends, may actually meet a couple's need for breathing space. She may be too preoccupied with her career to give close attention to the relationship, and his anxiety about total commitment may make him more comfortable being alone on weekday evenings. The geography of miles between them serves them well.

Closely related to the boundary between the spouses is the boundary that separates the couple from the rest of the world, including friends, careers, and families of origin. In fact, boundaries between two people (or groups) are always related to the boundaries around them. The more closely fused two people are to others, the less able they are to join together. Creating or strengthening the boundary around the couple requires that they separate themselves to some extent from former contacts and activities and from their separate families.

The degree of investment that each partner will have in the

marriage depends in part on how much is given up. Those who give up more may demand more from the relationship.

Women often seem to require more emotional commitment from marriage than men. Actually, this may have been more true formerly than it is now. The time is gone when we can ascribe this pattern to women's supposed dependency. Close inspection reveals that a woman who enters a traditional marriage does give up more. She is likely to put her own interests on hold or move away from friends and family according to the demands of a husband's job. These patterns may be changing, but twenty years ago it was natural for women to demand more of their marriages: they gave up more.

At the same time that couples are reducing their own previous contacts, both must add new contacts to join the partner's world. In-laws arrive on the scene. The number of relationships is increased, enriching but complicating the functioning of the new family system. Working out relations with the in-laws can be vexing, and it is a problem unique to our species. Other animals separate from their families when they mate; and if the truth be known, many people wish they could do the same.

No matter what is worked out, a couple must undergo a degree of separation from their families of birth, in order to establish a clear boundary around the new system in formation. If a young husband or wife remains enmeshed with his or her parents, their own boundary as a couple will be inadequate. Examples of people who have trouble exchanging the role of son or daughter for that of husband or wife are all too familiar. The son who spends every weekend repairing his parents' house won't have time to put his own house in order; the daughter who calls her mother every day and runs home when she and her husband have an argument won't learn how to solve problems in her marriage.

Members of the post-World War II generation expected their marriage vows to double as declarations of independence from their parents, but are often forced by economic conditions into prolonged dependency on their families. Many middle-class couples have to turn to their parents for "loans" in order to buy a house. No matter how hard they try to separate financial from emotional dependency, they find it impossible to feel truly emancipated as long as they know that they may have to turn to their parents in a pinch.

As in any system, relationships in families are interdependent. What happens between adult children and their parents will affect what happens in the marriage, and both of these boundaries will affect the boundary-making between the new couple and their own children.

The Party of the Third Part

The advent of a child—the party of the third part—adds a new dimension to family life, requiring the formation of even more boundaries. The man and woman are now parents; but in relationship to each other, they are—or can be—still a couple. Whether they maintain the vitality of this relationship or not depends to a large extent on the nature of the boundary they erect between themselves and their offspring.

Initially, the physical and emotional demands of infant children pull husband and wife away from each other. Because the connection between mothers and newborns is necessarily close and consuming, the boundary between the couple becomes wider. Some spouses greet the distancing with relief, others with regret. For a woman whose husband is aloof, children can fill an emotional void. For a husband who is accustomed to being number one around the house, there is now the maddening sense of coming in second: "Not now, honey; I have to feed the baby."

Children assert their needs with all the power of nature struggling for survival; their demands to be taken care of virtually force the couple to become parents and minimize (or fuse) the boundary between the two generations. When parental love and obligation are added to the equation, it is easy to see how the boundary demarcating the couple can erode. Yet husband and wife can be sustained as a loving couple and enhanced as parents if they reserve time for themselves. In a child-centered culture, some parents are slow to discover this. Worn out by their small charges and willing to put the child's needs before their own, they delay establishing the boundary that gives them some privacy *and* allows them as parents to assume a position of leadership.

Some couples rarely leave their children with babysitters and rarely go out alone together. Whatever they do, they do "as a family." What once was a couple becomes submerged in parenthood. This pattern makes for problems when the couple reaches midlife. By this time the children are growing up and developing interests of their own. They no longer want to be snared in the web of togetherness. Often with considerable struggle, they wriggle out, leaving their parents alone to face each other.

When this happens, many couples react like a tripod with the third leg pulled out: at best the system becomes unstable; at worst it topples. Over the years, many of us stabilize our relationships by diverting conflict to a third party; this process has been called *triangulation.* According to Murray Bowen, one of the founding parents of family therapy, the basic stable unit of an emotional system is the triangle. We may think of ourselves as involved in a number of two-person relationships

—a stable marriage, for example, or a lasting friendship—but closer examination usually reveals that these relationships are actually parts of a triangle.

Before long most two-person relationships run into some stress and anxiety, at which point it is automatic to triangle in a third person as a way of diverting the anxiety between the twosome. To illustrate: suppose you take a new job. At first you deal directly with your boss—ask for direction, make requests, and so on. When there is a conflict, you try to work it out. Say you need more material support to carry out your duties, but the boss disagrees. If the two of you agree to disagree—that is, if both of you can take a position and allow that the other one also has a legitimate position—then you may be able to keep the disagreement within the relationship (where it belongs). Often, however, in standing up for your own position, one or both of you will try to invalidate the other's. When this happens it is almost a reflex to triangle in someone or something. You might go home and gripe about the unreasonable boss, or complain to a co-worker, or take the afternoon off to commiserate over a few drinks. The problem is not so much complaining or seeking temporary relief, but the likelihood that these diversions will become a regular part of the relationship. Instead of bringing discussions with the boss (or your spouse, or a friend) to a conclusion, you are programmed to break off at a certain level of intensity.

It turns out that virtually all of our relationships are sustained as parts of a triangle. Moreover, we participate frequently in the process of other people's diversion. We are flattered when someone tells us a secret or confides in us about problems. Once in a while it is clear that we need to say, "You should tell that to her (or him)," but often we don't act on this.

Triangulation buys stability at the cost of failing to resolve key conflicts. Repeated many times, triangulation becomes a chronic pattern, preventing the resolution of differences and thereby robbing relationships of some of their potential for intimacy. The illusory harmony that a couple achieves by diverting most of their energy into their children may be shattered as the children grow up and move out.

When we try to expand our understanding of ourselves by taking into account our relationships, it is natural to think in dyadic (one-on-one) terms. If a woman of thirty-five is depressed and anxious, she may begin to think about relationships that may be depressing her. Perhaps she is worn out and frustrated by her children: they take for granted all that she does for them, always want more, and feel free to disobey her. But this is only part of the story.

This woman's relationship with her children, for example, is tied to her relationship with her husband (or other significant persons in her life). It does no good for her to try harder to discipline the children if their misbehavior is subtly encouraged by their father, and she will continue to be worn out by them if she and her husband are too distant to give each other support. To further complicate the picture, the system that is structured also includes work. The woman's relationship to her children is affected by her job as well as by the relationship to her husband (and his job). Workaholics of either sex may be enmeshed to work as much as if the job were a lover.

Triangulation relates to boundaries as process to structure. If a couple detours around their conflicts to focus on the children, they establish a family framework with a rigid boundary between the couple and a diffuse boundary between parents and children. Because these boundaries remain invisible we do not see the structure of our families any more than fish see the water they swim in. Nevertheless, we all act within the confines of our system. In this sense, the family is our goldfish bowl.

Family Rules

Systems theory enables us to understand the invisible limits imposed on our actions. Unseen forces begin to lose their power once we learn to see them. But it is hard to play a game, especially a complicated one, if you don't know the rules.

Not only are family systems structured, they are also characterized by organized sequences of behavior. These sequences —*family rules*—are originally products of our own creation, but over the years they endure as patterns that determine how and when and to whom family members relate. When a mother tells her daughter to pick up the toys and the child refuses until her father yells at her, an interactional pattern is initiated. If it works, it may be perpetuated as a family rule: mother is incompetent at setting limits, so father is the disciplinarian. The corollary is that mother becomes closer and more affectionate to the children, while father, the disciplinarian, moves to the outside.

Rules, such as the one above, are perpetuated even though they constrain the actions of family members. Since no one ratifies the rules, it is hard to examine them. Like the unconscious motives we considered in previous chapters, they owe their continuing sway over our lives to their covert status.

By the time we reach midlife, family rules are tenacious and resistant to change. Although alternatives are available, we are unlikely to consider them until extreme stress produces dysfunction in the system.

In order to understand how family rules work it is important to keep in mind that they describe *regularity* rather than regulation. A parent who wakes up a teenager and nags the child to get to school on time is operating according to a rule which says that the child's behavior is the parent's responsibility. This rule (more appropriate for younger children) frustrates the parent and prevents the teenager from becoming more responsible, but it does delay the necessity for parent and child to deal with a change in the nature of their relationship. Or consider the situation of a man who comes home from work each night too tired to exchange more than a few perfunctory remarks with his wife. Over the years, the couple has worked out rituals that preoccupy them while preventing long conversations that might lead to arguments. The unspoken rule is that they talk for a few moments; then each one gets involved with other things.

The trouble with unspoken rules is that when they no longer work, they are hard to talk about. Suppose the man above gets demoted at work and no longer finds satisfaction in his job. Now when he comes home, he wants more attention from his wife. But it is hard to change the rules. As the man tries to move closer to his wife, the children may pull harder on her, resisting any change in the triangle to which they have grown accustomed.

The concept of family rules was developed from observations of families in severe trouble. (Human nature is often easier to observe in pathological cases, where patterns of behavior are exaggerated in a caricature of normal life.) The strongest emotion in these families is fear—fear of the unknown, fear of the complex, and fear of change. What they want beyond all else is safety. Their anxiety inclines them to paralysis within narrow ranges of conduct. The sickest of them fight hardest to stay as they are—anything is better than change. We all have some of this, though we may not see it. We learn to walk around in our own worlds, within safe limits worked out over the years.

Women and men reaching midlife in the 1980s have a paradoxical relationship to family rules. On the one hand, changing roles for individuals exert pressure on the family to change; on the other hand, people under personal stress crave stability in their family lives. Today, single-parent families and two-paycheck families far outnumber the traditional arrangements, where one person worked while the other managed the home front. Now when a tired wage earner comes home, the partner—if there is one—is also likely to be a tired wage earner. People in stressful and demanding careers look more for security than satisfaction in their home lives. Home in the 1980s has become a place to pull yourself together in order to face work again tomorrow. This puts a premium on reducing tension and avoiding conflict, reinforcing the tendency to maintain predictable family rituals, even though they may be stultifying.

Another contemporary phenomenon that forces a growing number of men and women to confront boundaries and rules is the formation of stepfamilies. At the beginning of 1985, there were thirty-five million stepparents. No one has to tell a stepparent that families have protective membranes and their own special way of doing things. These people learn that they have to earn a place in the children's lives—a place not automatically accorded to them when they marry. Since 90 percent of the time it is the mother who gets custody after divorce, most of these new parents are stepfathers—and most of them are likely to hear, more than once, "You aren't my father!" A popular term for these reconstructed systems is "blended families"; my own experience more often reminds me of the old science fiction movie *When Worlds Collide*.

If the person in midlife does decide to make readjustments, the family system may resist. When we consider the fate of someone who tries to make a significant change in midlife, we often see only half the picture. Take, for example, the driven corporate executive who decides to slow down a bit and enjoy the pleasures of family life. Whether or not that person succeeds depends not only upon his or her conscious and unconscious relationship to work—can the person slow down?—but also upon whether the family will make room to draw the person in. We think of celebrated failures to relinquish the obsession to succeed—John DeLorean, Muhammad Ali—as being unable to let go of their quest for success. But what we don't know—and probably never know about public figures— is whether they could not let go of driving ambition because they were unable to take hold of family life.

Feedback is a technical concept that has crept into ordinary language, losing some of its original meaning in the process. Most people say "feedback" when they mean verbal criticism: "The instructor gave individual *feedback* to every participant, so that they could improve their performance for next time." This sort of evaluative commentary *is* feedback, but it is only the most obvious kind. As often with human dynamics, the more subtle forms of feedback turn out to be the most interesting—and powerful.

Feedback is a concept that originated with cybernetic theory. Developed in the late 1940s, this theory describes systems that regulate themselves using feedback loops. One example of a cybernetic system is the home heating unit, which is regulated by means of a thermostat that signals the furnace to operate until the ambient temperature reaches a preset point. Feedback, like family rules, functions to maintain homeostasis —not *in*variance, but stability in variance.

By introducing concepts of feedback and circular causality (mutual influence), cybernetic theory makes complex human phenomena predictable. Consider, for example, a father who intervenes whenever his children start to quarrel. Like most of us, the father may be trapped in the habit of linear thinking (their actions *cause* my actions). He believes that the children's yelling makes him intervene. By this reasoning, he is likely to keep trying to solve their problem by his actions. From the outside, however, we can see the same sequence as a self-perpetuating feedback loop: as soon as the children's emotional temperature rises, the father intercedes to cool them down. Unfortunately, in the process, they keep him involved—children learn to depend on adult interference—and he prevents them from learning to solve their own problems.

The cybernetic model is useful, but limited; it is mechanical, and people are not. The father in the previous example is not forever trapped in the cycle of intervention. He can raise his own acceptance of the children's arguing to a point where they will learn to settle most of their own problems. He can do so because, unlike machines, people are active and creative. If the father is sufficiently unhappy with his predicament, he can change his behavior or seek advice that will enable him to readjust the system. Alternatively, the children may be resourceful enough to realize that when they want to play (and argue) without interruption, they must do so out of earshot.

Human systems must grow and change; if they do not, members of the system may get stuck, frozen in patterns that have outlived their usefulness.

The Family Life Cycle

Hard as it is to describe systems, it is even more difficult to describe how they grow. Even experts on the subject often fall back upon the language of individual experience, making the family life cycle seem like nothing more than the parallel development of individuals. Midlife adults, for example, are said to have to adjust to changes in their children at the same time they are adjusting to their own middle age. Men are supposed to have special trouble accepting the growing power of their adolescent sons and the sexual maturing of their daughters. Women are expected to suffer an "empty nest" syndrome when their children move away. These descriptions are valid as far as they go, but they may not go far enough.

Fathers and mothers *do* have trouble letting their children grow up. But the reasons have as much to do with the resistance of systems to change as with the private conflicts of individuals. The challenge of adolescent change is the difficulty of realigning the boundary separating the family from the outside world. Mothers—central figures in the family and favorite targets of sociological critics—don't necessarily suffer when the nest is emptied; many find it a positive and liberating experience. Those women who do become depressed without their children are not necessarily dependent or inadequate. From a systems perspective, the empty nest syndrome—when it occurs—is a signal that the whole family needs to readjust from being a unit of three or four to being a unit of two. Often the problem is in the coalition between the parents, rather than inside either one of them.

In tracking the life cycle of family systems, there are several concepts that may be useful. The first is that family systems consist of at least three generations, so that problems in any one generation interact with problems in the other two. To understand the empty nest syndrome, for example, it may be necessary to consider the parents' relationships with their children, with each other, and with their own parents. A sterile marriage, career frustration, or trouble with the extended family all make it harder to deal with an adolescent's stormy passage.

Here the Freudian concepts of fixation and regression are useful in understanding families. Like individuals, families often get stuck at points of transition. When stressed, the family may revert to an earlier mode of functioning. This process of regression is illustrated in the following example.

In school Jesse excelled at everything but socializing. His parents were not surprised when he won a baseball scholarship to an Ivy League college or when he made dean's list in his second semester. They expected excellence from him and in fact would accept no less. They were surprised, however, when he became engaged to Carla.

Carla was a tall, dark Mediterranean beauty. She was also intelligent, Jesse's parents noted with approval. But Jesse did not; he saw only her looks. Being with this desirable woman made him feel special. Still, he never quite believed that he deserved her affection or that someone so obviously special could really love him. He was, therefore, intensely jealous and insisted that she concentrate her attention exclusively on him. Carla went along with this, seeing his jealousy as a sign of devotion and his vulnerability as evidence of a sensitive nature.

After they were married, things changed. Not Jesse's jealousy or his need for reassurance, but Carla's tolerance.

What changed? Carla? Not really. A more useful way to look at the problem is to see it as a problem of a system in transformation. The intense togetherness of courting couples generally must be modified after marriage to allow contact outside the relationship—with jobs, friends, and the wider family. Accommodating to changed status can take months—even years—and the process can be quite painful.

Jesse and Carla's first few years of marriage were fraught with conflict. They argued about one thing and another, but underneath was the fact that Jesse needed constant infusions of affection and reassurance, lest his inner insecurity reach the level of awareness. Finally, the couple reached an acceptable level of adjustment. Who changed? The system. When they added children to their family, Jesse and Carla stabilized their relationship. Children didn't solve their conflict, but they served as a focus for many of the feelings that could not be contained in the twosome. The children were the third leg of the triangle.

Carla quit work to look after the children; they both agreed that was best. As long as Carla was home, Jesse worried less that she might meet someone she liked better than him. Carla found that she now had the children, as well as Jesse, to fill up her life. Relieved to have put the awful fights behind them, Jesse and Carla let go of some of their utopian expectations of marriage and learned to enjoy a tolerably good relationship.

Fifteen years later they were divorced. What happened? When the children reached high school age, they were sent off to boarding school. Jesse wanted them to have the same advantages that he had had (besides, he was a little jealous of the attention Carla showed them). Shortly thereafter, Carla decided to go back to work. Jesse was all in favor. "She should have something to do," he thought; and, though he would never say so, he felt that she had become somewhat boring. Unfortunately, neither one of them realized that the change would put them right back where they started: an unstable unit of two. The fighting was awful, worse than before. Jesse was exquisitely jealous of anyone—male or female—Carla met at work; and she needed friends to fill the void left by the children's absence. Things fell apart in a hurry.

This family came apart in midlife because they remained fixated at an early level of adjustment—not as individuals, but as a system. Children didn't resolve the original conflict—they only served as a distracting detour. Once they left, things returned to the unhappy status quo of the early years. Only worse: now that they were approaching middle age, neither Jesse nor Carla could tolerate the conflict. They couldn't see it as an unsolved developmental problem, which might have given them the courage to stick it out. So they split up.

The crisis in midlife for Jesse and Carla can be understood from a number of perspectives, each with a piece of the truth and each with its own implications for resolution. Jesse's experience was of his wife pulling away from him, of terrible shame when she rejected his dependent longings, and finally of rage when she persisted in developing relationships outside the marriage. The problem, in Jesse's eyes, was Carla: "She couldn't make a commitment to the marriage." In his view, the solution was for her to change, to settle down and be the wife he needed.

For her part, Carla thought of Jesse as being unable to let go of the children, as not being able to tolerate their leaving home, and as desperately clinging to her instead of "growing up." He should, she believed, expand his own interests rather than try to contract hers. Each of them was a little bit right and a little bit wrong. The trouble is that solutions limited to what the other person should do seldom work.

Had they consulted a psychotherapist, Jesse or Carla might have been exposed to either one, or both, of two biases, depending on the therapist's training. The first is a tendency to equate personal fulfillment with the expression of an individual's feelings and conscious desires. In cases of marital conflict, this can lead to an inadvertent, but nonetheless powerful, push toward separation. The second bias is the idea that personality is set in childhood and that the outcome of adult life is largely dictated by early experience.

The life cycle approach to development, as I've indicated earlier, is more optimistic. It predicts and encourages growth and change in the adult years. According to this perspective, personality is set in childhood—but it is not set in concrete. To take this thought further, family development is more than the concurrent development of several people who happen to share the same household. The family is a system that goes through its own developmental cycle, modeling and molding its members.

Systems thinkers emphasize—perhaps overemphasize—homeostatic mechanisms, which protect the family structure from the vicissitudes of change. But families also grow and change. The family life cycle is a process of expansion and contraction, requiring periodic realignment of the system. This viewpoint does not solve the struggle to adjust to changes in midlife, but it helps clarify the process.

It is easier to see the family as a developing organic whole if we use a wide-angle lens. The ant marching through the forest in a column does not realize that it is part of a larger entity, capable of doing things, like crossing streams, that no single ant can do. The outsider sees it; the ant doesn't. The outsider, the naturalist, sees the unity of the system by standing back, ignoring the individuals in order to see the whole. When it comes to human systems, it takes creative imagination to stand back far enough to see the emergent processes of whole systems. Family theorists, naturalists on the human scene, have shown us how our own lives are shaped by patterned transactions that we don't often see and by relationships at which we don't often look.

When Jesse and Carla's children went off to school, boundaries that had remained stable for more than a dozen years suddenly had to become more elastic. The children's departure pulled out the third leg of the triangle propping up the unstable marital pair, who were forced to face each other again. Family stress is most acute at transition points like these, and we all have a tendency to get stuck in the painful process of accommodating to new circumstances.

Unfortunately, in the process of stepping back far enough to see the whole system, we risk losing sight of the individual. If people were billiard balls, their interactions could be understood solely on the basis of systemic forces. The difference is that human beings interact according to their conscious and unconscious expectations of each other. Some of these expectations are built up over the course of a couple's, or a parent and child's, history together. Others are ingrained in childhood. The forty-year-old woman who cringes when her husband criticizes her may be reacting not only to him and their history together, but perhaps also to internalized images of herself as the weak and dependent child of an unpredictable mother.

The billiard ball model of behavior does have its uses. It can help us to regulate family transactions in a way that minimizes destructive collisions. But the greater difficulty for many of us is coming together at all. The achievement of loving relationships is the major self-expressive activity of the total person. Unfortunately, many of us reach midlife with a complex inhibition of the capacity to love and be loved. Even the most "self-sufficient" of us may have an unconscious, long-standing, unsatisfied need for love, which comes to the surface at times of safe distance. One woman I know is regularly flooded with love for her children when she is away on business trips. Another person cries for lost love during sweetly sad melodramas. The love that these people yearn for is available. They hang back because they are afraid of intimacy.

The Fear of Intimacy

Membership in a family system is not optional. Participation is. We are molded at an early age in the families of our birth and continually defined by family relations in our adult years.

Still, some people minimize their participation in family life. Careerists spend most of their time at work, middle-aged athletes use up their energy running or playing tennis, and many people give up trying to maintain personal relationships with their parents as a lost cause.

It is important to realize our connection to others and to participate as fully as possible in human relations. But there is a catch. Some people can't. Or, to put it more accurately, each of us has a limited tolerance for closeness. When we overstep these limits we get anxious and run. The anxiety can be overcome, but not by ignoring or denying it. We can influence others, but we can only do so by changing ourselves; and we cannot change ourselves in important ways without a struggle over our inner fears of closeness.

People who isolate themselves may not even feel lonely. Loneliness means active longing for people. The feeling hurts, but it's a feeling of life. Isolated people are alone, but do not feel it. A sad example of this was a patient who spent all his time avoiding his wife and children. He thought they were trying to engulf him, sap his energy, submerge him, load him up with responsibility, and cheat him out of freedom, peace, and pleasure. All they really wanted was to love him.

This man, who appeared so detached, just couldn't tolerate closeness. Those who resist intimacy the most are those who are most afraid of getting swallowed up in relationships. The self-sufficient introvert, only loosely connected to family and friends, may appear to have lost the capacity to love. These people are able to love, but afraid—afraid of people, afraid of love, afraid of demands, afraid of impingement—so they distance themselves from others in order to avoid the danger of being treated coldly, unempathically, or with hostility. They develop the habit of staying away, not from everyone, but from those with the capacity to hurt them. The distancing is based on a correct assessment of their sensitivity to criticism or rejection. Isolation, instituted as a defense, becomes a habit.

We move through life in a protective bubble of psychological distance. We learn at an early age how close we can get without being anxious, and then we establish our relationships at that distance. We lose sight of the protective distance, because we rarely bridge it. We preoccupy ourselves with other things. And whatever dissatisfactions we feel seem to be caused by those around us. "Distancers" experience people who would get close as dependent and smothering. "Pursuers" don't have to confront their own problems with intimacy as long as they keep pursuing others, pushing them farther away in the process. Beneath the apparent differences, pursuers and distancers are both afraid of intimate relationships.

When early experience has confirmed that we are lovable and that others are loving, then we can approach life with confidence. Otherwise, we may always be reaching for a special relationship, one with the magic to heal emptiness. When we look for the "ideal relationship," we are looking for someone who allows us to express ourselves completely, without opposition or criticism.

People remember with longing the strong feelings of being "in love." Some find this delicious infatuation again in extramarital relationships. It's wonderful, but it isn't love. Not yet. Comparing this intoxication with the everyday emotions of marriage leads to many mistakes. In hot desire, passionate coming together alternates with separation and longing. Fond longing from a distance is not the same as love sustained. Nor is it love to need always to be with someone, to be uneasy apart and only feel safe together. Real love means closeness between two people who remain separate. There is a wanting to give and a willingness to take, but not a needy, symbiotic fusion. Adult love is sustained intimacy between two complete selves.

What happens when we bring buried and forgotten emotions out of hiding? We are once again vulnerable to the same forces responsible for pushing them away in the first instance. We become so sensitive to criticism, disapproval, and rejection that we, ourselves, become our own harshest critics. In maturity we can anticipate some hurt as we experiment with intimacy; only now, instead of shrinking back, we can begin to accept and understand it. Learning to love is a process of looking in and reaching out.

8

Kinship and Friendship

By the time we reach middle age, most of us have cooled off the emotional heat of relations with parents and siblings. We take it as a sign of growth to separate from our parents, and we measure our maturity by independence of family ties. Yet many of us still respond to our families as though they were radioactive and capable of inflicting great pain. Only one thing robs Superman of his extraordinary power: kryptonite, a piece of his home planet. A surprising number of adult men and women are similarly rendered helpless by even a brief visit to or from their parents.

Only when they get far enough away from their families— out of range of the radiant heat—do some people feel safe enough to think fondly of their kin. Of course, they may feel periodic surges of longing for lost family ties. The telephone company's slogan, "Reach out and touch someone," capitalizes on this universal desire for connection. (The telephone is an instrument well suited to controlled and limited contact, because it is a cooler vehicle of encounter than face-to-face meet-ings.) With the help of the florist industry, we have even institutionalized reconnecting with our parents and other rela-tives on special days. But artificial occasions like Mother's Day and Father's Day only serve to disguise the reality of loosened family bonds.

A number of social trends have conspired to make the lives of Americans in the 1980s uniquely difficult and increasingly alienated. Decline of the extended family, the epidemic of divorce, economic pressure, and the lost art of friendship have affected most of us, at least to some extent. The mobility of American workers is also blamed for the erosion of family relations. People reading this book may have moved half a dozen times since leaving home as young adults. It is of course hard to maintain close contact with families when they live hundreds of miles away. Mobility *does* separate people from their families of origin, but it may be more an effect than a cause of family alienation.

Not everyone moves away from home. A minority, bound by ties to the community, stay close. Some are apparently success-ful at forging a separate identity and also maintaining genuine involvement with their families. More often, however, the togetherness syndrome that controls the lives of these people constricts their development as individuals. They don't choose to stay close to home; they are stuck. As children these people were held too close too long by jealous and dependent parents. Having become objects of intense and suffocating parental devotion, they remain tethered, not freely joined.

Even the majority who flee their families are seldom really free. Distance and infrequent contact afford them the illusion that they are grown up, but it is primarily an illusion. If they left home somewhere around age eighteen, childhood relation-ships were still being transformed to an adult basis. But because they leave, the transition may never have been completed. Even when the "children" are thirty or forty, their relationships to their parents remain frozen in adolescent patterns. Superman becomes mortal in contact with kryptonite; mortals become teenagers in contact with their parents.

The point is that few of us have mature, intimate relationships with our parents. Those who move away and visit infrequently are likely to have cordial but superficial contact; they are independent only at a distance. Those who stay close are often equally unable to be themselves in relation to their parents; they have more time with their parents but not necessarily more intimacy. They are near but not close.

The Family Legacy

Of the many people who acknowledge the turmoil they feel during family visits, only a few recognize their own contribution. Most blame their parents: it is the parents who didn't change or grow up. This factor has special significance. As long as people remain emotionally hyperreactive to their parents, they will also be hyperreactive to people in their adult lives who push the same buttons their parents did. The same individuals whose parents "never grew up" are likely to be surrounded by other people who "didn't grow up."

In psychoanalysis this is called transference. But the tendency to react to others as though they represented unresolved relationships from the past is not confined to any one situation. The patient in the following account did not recognize this pattern when he came to see me at age thirty-five for psychotherapy. Like many people, he masked his emotional vulnerability to his parents with distance, the same distance he used to protect himself from other people in his adult life.

As a second child, Michael had been close to both parents.

With his mother he shared the everyday experiences of a child's life; with his father he shared a deep love for the out-of-doors. Michael's father was a transplanted New Yorker who cherished everything green. Together father and son went fishing, and although the trips occurred no more than two or three times a year, they were long-anticipated and long-remembered.

When Michael became a teenager the fishing trips stopped; or, to be exact, Michael stopped going. He developed a healthy case of adolescent rebellion. Nothing his father did was right. According to Michael, his father wasn't cool (he cried in the movies); he was no John Wayne; he didn't like sports; he was excessively polite; and he was not permissive. In short, he was a total failure. So Michael turned away from his father and transferred his hero worship to idols of the culture. (Another feature of his alienation was invisible to Michael then and when I saw him: by rejecting his father, he became the secret ally of his mother's covert hostility toward the father.)

At college (a college Michael's mother favored and his father opposed), a remarkable thing happened: his father grew up, or so it seemed to Michael. Maybe his dad wasn't John Wayne (nobody's perfect), but as Michael's interests shifted from action to ideas, he discovered that his father wasn't such an old fogey after all. Except for Michael's brief visits home they still didn't see each other much, but distance apparently healed the breach in Michael's heart.

During his twenties, Michael's sights were fixed on success. His preoccupation with "making it" was not unique, but it seemed to operate in him with special force. Driven by an unaccountably strong fear of failure and inspired by images of great accomplishment, his dreams were endless.

Marriage was not on Michael's conscious agenda, until meeting the right person changed his plans. His driving ambition remained, but he did make room in his life for a wife and family. Not right away, however, and not easily; his wife and children had to assert their claim on him, and he had to learn that becoming a husband and a father takes time and effort.

During those years of uneasy transition, Michael saw more and more of his father. The two men turned to each other and became sources of mutual support and confidence. The special pleasure they took in each other's company was almost too good to be true. "What an idiot I was as a teenager," Michael thought; "I really have a wonderful father." At the same time, the glow he felt toward his father warmed his inner image of himself.

For all the enjoyment they had together, Michael and his father still saw each other infrequently. The problem was time. As long as professional success seemed uncertain but possible, he could not emancipate himself from his six and a half–day workweeks. There would be time later. "Someday . . ." he rationalized.

A phone call from his mother—"Your father is dying"— brought Michael home immediately. The following week was one of those supercharged times when something basic suddenly becomes clear. The possibility of his father's death sank in and with it the awareness that his own time was limited.

Michael's father did not die, though it tooks months before he resumed full participation in life. When Michael thought his father was well enough, he proposed that the two of them take off for a week of fishing. It would be the trip they had always dreamed of—a whole week—and it would be a celebration of the father's return to health. For Michael, who was now in psychotherapy, it would also be an opportunity to get to know his father, and in the process himself.

Father and son set off for Canada. They rented a cabin in a remote fishing camp on a small lake. In this rustic setting, there were few luxuries; they looked forward to getting along without electricity, telephones, and newspapers. For one week they would be alone with the trees, the loons, the trout—and each other.

The first three days were perfect. They fished from first light until late afternoon. Then they sat on the porch of their cabin, drinking beer, watching the sun sink into the horizon, and talking. They talked past news and current events, past family gossip and goings on at work, until they got to the things that mattered most to them. They talked about private concerns— the father's fears of dying, Michael's ambitions and his shyness —and they talked about their relationship. They spoke of their long alienation; and they said what men rarely say, that they loved each other.

After the first three days, Michael learned to ignore the mosquitoes, but he couldn't ignore his father's annoying habits. Now he remembered what drove him crazy as a teenager. It was his father's preoccupation with himself. When he listened to Michael, he only half-listened, waiting to change the subject to himself, his problems, and his accomplishments. And what hurt most was that when they were talking at dinner in the main lodge, his father would interrupt their conversation to talk with anyone else who happened to be near—a new audience for his stories about himself. This discovery was especially painful to Michael because he could see how his sensitivity to his father's lack of concern was what kept him from opening up to other people.

His wife, for example. She really did care about him, really was interested in what he had to say. But whenever she allowed the children to interrupt or answered the phone while Michael was talking, it evoked a deep-seated feeling that no one really cared about him. He might have told her, but his hurt and anger was too immense. If he did tell her, she might have trouble understanding; after all, she was only listening to the kids and picking up the phone. So instead of expressing his feelings, he told himself that she didn't care and he was never again going to open himself to the hurt of rejection by talking about what was really important to him.

Other people in Michael's life irritated his sensitivity to rejection in different ways, but he responded in the same way he had learned to as a child—that is, he felt hurt and angry, yet powerless to do anything but withdraw. He avoided his boss, because the boss seldom praised him; he avoided talking to people at parties because when they asked about him he felt their interest was shallow and insincere. His standoffishness was only a device to protect his bruised feelings, although he recognized that tolerating the risk of rejection was a necessary survival mechanism in close-range relationships.

Michael's experience was unique only in that he began to see how he avoided in friends and colleagues precisely those things he found annoying in his father. Marriage shields many people from their parents, but those like Michael who marry without resolving that relationship usually recapitulate the same emotional reactivity with their mates. Until we learn to relate as adults to our parents, we remain forever vulnerable to habits of adolescent overreaction. Until people stop running from their parents they have trouble getting close—and staying close—to anyone else.

The continuing influence of our families of origin is far-reaching and pervasive. We are guided in what we do by what our parents did. Sometimes we recall: "They took separate vacations, and that seemed to work out, so why don't we try it?" Or: "They made me go to Sunday school and I hated it;

so I'm not going to subject my kids to that malarkey." More often, we don't remember; we just feel compelled to do things in a certain way—and it just happens to be the same way they did them. (You may notice this more readily in your spouse or a friend than in yourself—*they* do so many things just the way their parents did.) When we do become aware of duplicating our parents' habits, we often feel trapped in our genes: "My God, I'm growing up to be my mother!"

Most of the adaptive habits and traits that are passed on from our parents become unrecognized, inherent features of character. Psychoanalysts call those features of personality that we take for granted "ego syntonic," in contrast to "ego alien" characteristics, which stick out as annoying appendages. Ego alien habits are often maddeningly inflexible, but at least we can see them and therefore try to do something about them.

Unfortunately, some people are so busy not being their parents that there is no room left to be themselves. Actively struggling to *not* be your parents is the same game as being your parents. In either case, your life is run by them. There isn't much difference between a woman who feels she has to stay home with her small children because her mother did and one who absolutely refuses to consider doing what her mother did. Most of us are like our parents (usually more like one than the other). As soon as we stop fighting it, we can say, "Okay, I'm like my mother." Ironically, that is the way to be free to be yourself.

Like other creatures of nature, human beings are programmed to fight or flight when faced with danger. Since fighting with their parents seems like a losing proposition, many people take flight. Those having the most to work out are the ones least willing to try. Oh, they visit all right, but often the contact rubs tender spots, and so visits become less frequent and meetings are cushioned by always making sure that at least three people are present. Hiding behind the television set or the grandchildren accomplishes about the same thing as being too busy to write or visit. To be alone with either parent is to risk hurt and disappointment, and who needs any more of that?

Some of the saddest people I know stood over a parent's graveside, unable to say goodbye because they never really got to know each other, never became friends, never forgave, never apologized. A forty-three-year-old woman I spoke with recently said, "My father never told me he loved me," and she couldn't get over it. Everyone has an immense, an extraordinary capacity to love. The only thing that is bound up in our lives is the expression of that capacity. This woman's father loved her—he just couldn't put it into words.

Continued emotional divorce from the family of origin also produces unhealthy marriages and unhealthy children. Couples, too much together, give up interests that don't dovetail and thus deny parts of themselves. Michael's wife didn't like hiking and camping, so he gave it up. Michael didn't enjoy classical music, so his wife stopped going to concerts. Both were diminished in the process. When young families cut themselves off from kin and community they suffer from emotional overload, expecting more satisfaction from the small circle of intimates than it can provide.

Being trapped at close quarters places a premium on predictability. We get used to each other and pressure our partners to stay the same. The longer the relationship lasts, the more secure we feel. The emotions of jealousy and anger are subdued, but when we block feelings, we deaden experience. Numerous psychotherapies have sprung up to teach people to feel more, but as long as they are closeted in isolated families it remains dangerous to feel too much. The resulting brittleness is one reason so many families break up.

Even when two people divorce, they carry with them a legacy of unresolved sensitivities. Distance takes the heat off, but it doesn't put out the fire.

Friendship

The same vulnerability that keeps people at arm's length from their families limits emotional connections outside the family. Few middle-aged adults have many friends, least of all mobile, middle-class professionals. Unlike working-class people rooted in the same ethnic communities they grew up in, the upwardly mobile lack the stability that enables them to maintain child-hood friendships. Those who work for large corporations don't stay in one place long enough to plant a garden much less reap a friendship. The not-so-funny joke among IBM families is that the initials stand for "I've been moved."

In childhood, opportunities for friendship come automati-cally. Children are thrown together at school and on the play-ground. Not everyone is popular, but most kids have at least a few friends. They don't have to work at it, so they don't learn how. Most people form their most intimate friendships at school. If they are lucky enough to stay close, then the friend-ship lasts; more often than not only the illusion of these rela-tionships is maintained, courtesy of the U.S. mails and the telephone company.

After leaving school, adults are rarely thrown together with such a large group of potential friends. The best chances to meet people are at work and in the neighborhood. Friendships do develop from these everyday encounters, but they are com-plicated by competing interests and other demands.

It starts with getting married. She sees less and less of her best friend, because her husband doesn't like her. She likes his old buddy; it's the buddy's wife she can't stand. Gradually they drift apart.

Becoming a parent makes it harder to be a friend. Children, conceived in the urge to expand, contract the family to center on their needs. Families with small children progressively retreat from old friends—unless they too have children. Taking care of children, which is always a demanding job, is twice as hard in a culture where nuclear families are isolated from kin. Preoccupied with the demands of small children, many parents are dulled by a long season of regression and too worn out to be very sociable.

Young mothers can, and wisely do, clan together for practical and emotional support. Their conversations may have more to do with Pampers than politics, but sharing these intimate details of everyday life draws them close. Close, but not always deep. The neighbor with small children will be able to recommend a pediatrician. But the odds are against her sharing enough interests, outside the children, to become a lasting friend.

The depth of friendship is hard to measure. Some people get together often, and they talk about a lot of things, perhaps even share confidences. Still, there is always a measured distance. Other would-be friends spend less time together, but when they do meet something special happens. They open themselves and feel close. But the closeness is time-limited. Their meetings are bound on either side by other things they consider more important. If you are expected home at the end of the day, you may have to confine your friendship to occasional lunches. Most families, especially young families, jealously guard their time together in the evening. Working late, going to a PTA meeting, maybe exercising—these are considered legitimate excuses to be absent from the family hour; spending time with a friend is probably not.

One measure of the depth of friendship is what the friends talk about. Friends may talk about the weather, national news, or clothes with pleasure and interest. Yet even when they limit the conversation to externals, they are sustained by the knowledge that they *can* go deeper—get down—to themselves and the relationship. When they want to, friends can be a closed system, complete, rather than two legs of a triangle that needs some other point of focus to stabilize it. Most of us have at least some relationships where we can talk about me and about you. If I am depressed, discouraged, I can talk about it; if you are, I can listen. The next step, talking about the relationship, is rarer. If you have a relationship with someone in which, when something is bothering you, you can say so, then you have a friend. (Psychotherapists know this, and the really good ones use the relationship as the fulcrum of change.)

Another measure of friendship is what you don't talk about. If you are lucky, you may have a friend in your husband or wife. But there are certain subjects in almost any marriage that the spouses don't talk about. Sometimes they are the things that trouble us most. We may not want to burden our spouse with financial problems (or may not want to share the decision-making). Maybe we can't admit to wanting time alone for ourselves. It's not necessarily a question of keeping secrets, though most husbands and wives have a few. Rather it's simply hard to live with someone and tell that person everything.

Some things won't be of interest, and over the years you learn to avoid boring each other. Other things just aren't worth the risk of disrupting the relationship. We may be too embarrassed to talk about our fears of inadequacy and too afraid of hurting (or provoking) the spouse to bring up certain complaints.

With friends it is possible to talk about everything—no holding back. That's the ideal, anyway. Few people may have such an ideal friend, one to whom they can say anything. But it is not unlikely to be able to do so with the aggregate of one's friends. The more the merrier—a variety of friends enables us to express a variety of parts of ourselves.

We are enriched by every good relationship, but because it takes a lot of effort to make and keep them, we have a tendency to expect too much from those we do have. One of the burdens on modern marriage is that diminishing ties to the extended family have not been compensated for by expanding friendships. The nuclear family is our nest and emotional headquarters, but asking it to meet all of our needs is asking too much. At certain stages of our lives, we tend to focus so much energy on one interest or one relationship, that we let ourselves become unbalanced, as was the case with Bob.

Bob called me for an appointment two weeks after his fortieth birthday. "I don't think it's anything serious," he said; "it's just that I've been blue for a couple of weeks and I can't seem to shake it." He didn't know exactly what was bothering him, and *that* was really what bothered him the most.

Bob described himself as a "straight-ahead guy," and he was. What he called "being blue" was a painful depression, but he didn't talk much about his feelings. Instead he went straight ahead to examine his life—like the good administrator: first find the problem, then apply the solution. He described his life systematically. Everything seemed to be in order. Things were going well at home, and at work things were better than okay. I asked him, "When did you first start feeling blue?" (careful to use his own metaphor). "Gee, I don't know; I guess it was right after my birthday party. It was my fortieth birthday, and

I was really looking forward to it. But when the guests showed up, I felt an awful letdown, and it's been getting worse ever since."

Something about turning forty, something about the party, seemed to hold the key to Bob's problem, but it wasn't until several sessions later that I finally realized what it was.

Turning forty meant reaching his peak. For some people this event stirs thoughts of growing old; for Bob it meant that he could now enjoy himself. What happened at the birthday party that so depressed him was that even after everybody showed up, he still felt alone. Like a lot of us, Bob hadn't made time for friendship. Now he had the time, but no friends.

In college, Bob had the most intense friendship of his life. He met Ed at football practice, and they were immediately drawn together. They both played linebacker, and they were good enough to be on athletic scholarships, but, unlike most of the other athletes they knew, neither one of them was a jock. They were bright, serious students, definitely kindred spirits.

As their friendship developed the two men were repeatedly delighted to find that they shared so many special interests. Bob had known other people who liked jazz, read the *New York Times*, and went to foreign films. But not too many other students seemed to share more than a few of his interests, and those who did were definitely not athletes. So he had two circles of friends—some he played ball with, some he talked about serious things with. Ed was the first friend who bridged both worlds.

In addition to playing football and going to classes, Bob worked part-time as a short-order cook. But he still found plenty of time to be with Ed. There was nothing deliberate or self-conscious about it. They liked each other, so they made time for their friendship. A lot of the things they did were active—going places, doing things—but the best times were the long conversations in the student union. As he talked about those times, I could see that Bob had the capacity for deep friendship—he could listen and he was loyal. He listened, not just waiting his turn to talk, but thinking about what was being said, taking it all in, and then answering honestly and from the heart. This is a rare talent, a deep attentivenesss and positive regard for people.

In his senior year Bob met Diane, and she became the center of his life. Bob still saw Ed, sometimes with Diane and occasionally alone. But after graduation when they moved to different cities, it was harder to keep in touch. There were too many other things, essential things, that came first.

Bob still considers Ed his friend, and there is no sense debating that. But, friends or not, they see each other only once every three or four years. Since college, there have been a handful of other people who might have become friends, but none of the relationships got very far. Bob had a wide circle of acquaintances, yet none of these satisfied the need for deep friendship.

The intensity required for deep friendship is precisely what we learn to mute in adolescence. In fact, that may be one of the most important lessons of growing up: don't feel too much; it isn't practical and you can get hurt.

After years of hiding sensitive feelings, the capacity for feeling itself begins to atrophy. By the time we wake up in midlife, longing for deeper alliances, a lot stands in the way: other calls on our time, the cultivated practical reserve, and beneath that a fear of intimacy. Bob's story turned out to be sadly typical, as he described how often he would shrink away from closeness. At first, it was the pressure of other commitments; eventually it became habit. He remembered thinking that people who stood around chatting were frivolous; he always had something to do.

Somewhere in his thirties he discovered that it was hard for him to relax his guard enough to let people in, even when he wanted to. It was a strange and uncomfortable feeling. Something as simple as being friendly—something he used to have to work at *not* doing—now was the hardest thing in the world for him. Solitude was a habit, supported by numerous well-practiced devices for keeping people away. At work, Bob ate lunch with a book to keep him company. On the train, he tried his best to fill up two seats, and when that wasn't possible he buried his face in a newspaper. These are common habits; what bothered Bob so much was his realization that he organized much of his life around avoiding people and that he now found it difficult to let down his barrier.

Men, Women, and Friends

In their studies of the adult life cycle, Daniel Levinson and George Vaillant found that few men make time for friends. Friendship doesn't have a sufficiently high priority in their already crowded lives. The economist Fred Hirsch observed that declines in friendship and friendliness are characteristic of modern economies. With dry wit he points out that friendliness "is time consuming and thereby likely to be economized because of its extravagant absorption of this increasingly scarce input." Hirsch suggests that the problem is most pronounced for people who are well-off and who set a higher valuation on their time. As a result, friendship and mutual concern are reduced in a society that becomes more concerned with material goods and even more pressed for time.

Women seem to have more friends than men. The women's movement served to legitimize and strengthen the solidarity among women, but it has always been easier for women than for men to enjoy friendship. The thing that changed was their recognition of the value of female friendships. As women began to think of male cultural tradition as their enemy, some turned even more to each other for support. In the seventies, cooperative, supportive relationships among women were advanced, creating a feeling of "sisterhood," which often translated into specific friendships. Women took strength from these bonds and freed themselves from the enslaving illusion that relationships with men are the only ones that really matter. No longer does the average woman think of herself only in relation to the men in her life. She is a person in her own right, free to pursue friendships with women and men.

Women are probably more free than men; women know the value of relationships and they are better at the art of relating. Women in friendship are open and nurturing; they talk freely and listen with interest. Women friends are comfortable with a wide range of subjects, from everyday domestic issues to more weighty subjects. Women together are not likely to be on guard; once they get to know each other, they rarely seem interested in scoring points or making an impression.

Stuart Miller, author of the excellent *Men and Friendship*, says that not having friends is peculiarly a man's problem. Many women think so too. My own impression is that women have more friends than men, but that the differences are exaggerated. In my experience, midlife is a time when men and women alike become keenly aware of the relative lack of friendship in their lives. Both genders have special limits that hold them back.

Among men, friendships tend to be "instrumental" (a concept from social psychology, meaning goal-oriented), rather than "expressive." Men play games together, watch sports on TV, talk about work, and may share hobbies. Commonly, men look to women, often their wives, to share their feelings. Men somehow have trouble shaking the dormant idea of other men as potential adversaries. And for this reason it is particularly hard for them to admit weakness, vulnerability, or even their raw ambition.

The fear of tenderness is reinforced, at least for most men, by a fear of homosexuality. The notion still persists that if you get too close to another man you may be taken as a homosexual —or worse, become one. The recent liberalization of social attitudes toward homosexuals hasn't done much to mitigate the anxieties of middle-aged men. To protect themselves, men are distant or act tough with one another. Backslapping, rough jokes, always ready to score points—there's not much softness in most male friendships. The fear of being "queer" is a screen, a shock symbol, for a more general fear of intimacy, a fear of touching.

The fear of sexual complications is probably more of an impediment to friendships between men and women. It may be easier for men to talk to women, to be friendly, even confide in them, but they are afraid to get too close. They are always a little careful, reserved, holding back. Their fear—fantasy— is that once the dam of repression breaks, the friends will be swept off to bed. And sometimes it happens.

There is much discussion these days about what kinds of relationships can exist between men and women. Since the balance of the sexes has changed radically, there have been new problems; there have also been new opportunities. As women and men become more equal in the workplace, the opportunity for friendship between the sexes increases. Younger men and women have less of a barrier between them. They made friends in coed college dormitories, and learned to be pals when going out in groups replaced pairing off as the major form of adolescent dating. But most of us now at midlife aren't so used to crossing the gender line for friendship. When we do, men may benefit more than women. Men talk, or so it is said, and women listen.

A lot of men are breaking out of the stereotype that once programmed them to limit conversation with other men to business, sports, and politics. But some men still find it easier to unburden themselves to a sympathetic woman friend. Single men and women learn a lot about the opposite sex from such friendships. A man may ask a woman friend Freud's famous question, "What do women want?" A woman may learn from a male friend how men feel pressured by some of the things women do. Years of indoctrination about sex roles may influence these relationships. Some men have difficulty overcoming the habit of thinking of women as either maternal figures or sex objects. Some women have difficulty overcoming their conditioning to subdue themselves in order to please men.

Our willingness to change is tied to our (own) security and support (from friends). One of the virtues of friendship is that friends help us to express underdeveloped aspects of our personalities. Few men change their mode of relating to women without women friends who are similarly committed, and few women change without at least partially cooperative men. It takes two to tango.

The beauty of friendship, wherever and whenever it exists, is that it is based not on need, but enjoyment and trust. Part of the charm of friendship is that it lacks the compulsion and possessiveness of romantic love. Yet, lacking the biological imperative and the rules that safeguard it, friendships are easier to neglect. Maintaining friendships means giving them priority; you *do* have to work at seeking out relationships and deepening them.

Like young mothers, career women, too, are drawn together. Theirs is the common bond of voyagers exploring new territory, where the natives (men) are tolerant but suspicious. Women seem better able to share their experience; they are more focused on sharing than competing.

A thirty-five-year-old professional woman wrote to tell me what role friendship plays in her life. Her letter illustrates some of the finest qualities of friendship. The best friendships are flexible, instrumental, *and* expressive. Listening, nonjudgmental friends, like those in the following narrative, can put therapists out of business.

"I just got back from four days with my best friend. This relationship has been going on for fifteen years. Elaine and I have spent hours supporting each other, pushing, yelling, depending, loving, eating, and shopping our way into middle age. We have gone through divorce (mine, then hers), death of both parents (hers), infidelity (both of us), childbirth (hers), remarriage (hers, then mine), undergraduate and graduate school (both of us), poverty (both), affluence (mostly hers), weight gain (a central issue for women and a never-ending topic for discussion), decorating our houses . . . fifteen years of focusing on the big events and the petty details.

"I tell her my horrible secrets and, as you say, your friends just like you. We spent all last weekend talking about how she'd like to obliterate her son who has just returned home, unemployed, uneducated, and expecting to be welcomed with open arms. 'You never really loved me,' he whined at the dining room table, as his mother gritted her teeth and rolled her eyes and said, 'Pam, do something or I'm going to kill him right here.'

"Maybe this all goes back to the kind of relationship women wanted with mothers, but whatever the reason, with Elaine I am accepted, understood, and sometimes mothered . . . and I also accept, understand, and mother.

"I don't think this is at all unusual. Lots of women I know who do not define themselves as feminists spend lots of time really talking to other women . . . sharing (what a trite word, but that's in fact what it is) the small details that add up and become overwhelming. Details about husbands and kids, and how the checker at the grocery store acted, and, more recently, what it feels like to be a boss or a surgeon, and the new favorite concern 'What will I wear to give my paper?'—something one would probably not discuss with male colleagues. We sit in each other's kitchens and tend to the adult equivalents of scraped knees, and cheer triumphs and gossip. At least that's what it's like for me and most of the women I know. Maybe because none of us expected to do anything other than get married and make babies, we were socialized into this comforting cadence of nurturing other people. Damned if I know.

"Something else is beginning to happen. At least it's being reported by what Nora Ephron calls 'the ladies central' (that informal group around the kitchen table). Middle-aged men do seem to want these kinds of relationships. The intimacy, the comfort . . . unfortunately, they also seem to be confusing that with sexuality. The women I know are capable of extending their particular kind of friendship to men, but the men often seem to get overwhelmed and think they're in love. I hear this over and over. I think it's interesting and I suppose it has to do with male midlife focus on reestablishing interpersonal ties. And I think the kind of friendship women offer is a truly remarkable thing and probably feels fantastic to someone who hasn't been paying much attention for twenty years."

The Shifting Balance of Relationships

As we have seen, our lives are balanced between relationships inside and outside the family. The fewer friends we have the more dependent we are on our families. This much is obvious. What may be less obvious is that this balance shifts. When we are forming new families, we reduce contact with our parents and friends. Later, as our children grow and no longer consume our lives, we may need to readjust the balance. Those who aren't aware of the need to change may have trouble locating the cause of their distress or, as in the following example, may protest that the family is letting them down.

Symptoms, not unhappiness, brought Sandy (married fifteen years) to psychotherapy. She was the one who called, and because she asked to be seen alone, I agreed, even though the fights she mentioned sounded like a family problem. (When families have problems, women often end up as "the patient." Husbands are ready to project responsibility and many women are ready to take it.) Ten minutes into the session I was convinced that I had been right in the first place. Most of Sandy's complaints were about her husband. "He's too wrapped up in himself and his job. He never has enough time for me." This is a common complaint among newly married couples, not so common after fifteen years, unless something changes, unbalancing the previous equilibrium.

Sandy had recently started working again, after staying home to take care of the children. I assumed that something about her going back to work was putting a strain on the marriage. Maybe Paul, her husband, was threatened by her independence. Perhaps she needed more help with the kids, and he wasn't willing. When I asked her to bring him to the next session, she said he probably wouldn't come. "He doesn't really care about me. Besides, he thinks going to a psychologist is a waste of time."

She was half right. Paul made no attempt to hide his disdain for psychotherapy ("People have to take care of their own problems; no one can do it for them"). But he did care about his wife, and he was concerned about what was happening to the marriage.

Professionals know that it isn't *what* people say, but *how* they say it—the quality of their interaction, not the content. The measure of communication is not politeness and affection, but whether or not the partners can keep talking, without giving up, breaking off, or bringing someone else into the discussion. Two people can yell back and forth in total disagreement, but if they keep talking they are communicating.

Sandy and Paul kept talking all right. They disagreed about the problem, but they both said what they thought *and* they both listened. She said that since she had gone back to work he didn't give her enough attention. He said that he was just as involved as ever; she just wasn't satisfied anymore.

As it turned out, when Sandy was home with the children, she felt her life was full. Still, by the end of the day she was glad to have Paul's company. He didn't help much around the house, but they did talk, about his day and her day. It was enough. So what changed? Now she had a job that she liked, and she had the same kind of relationship with Paul. But it wasn't enough. The missing factor was friendship.

Previously, Sandy had an elaborate network of friends, the modern suburban equivalent of an extended family. But when she resumed paid work, she lost that network. There seemed no opportunity for socializing during the day, nor was there the luxury of long visits after work.

Once Sandy realized this, she starting making time for her

friends, even enlarging her circle. As a result, her own life became more diverse, flexible, and satisfying. And, as often happens, change in one sphere had positive ramifications in others. Her new friendships enriched her relationship with Paul. Now when she came home from work there was much more to talk about.

Secrets of the Heart

One cannot account for the vicissitudes of relationships without also taking into account the vicissitudes of narcissism—our tender self-images warn us away from risking intimacy. When we do reveal the secrets of the heart, they are carefully selected. The more narcissistically vulnerable among us go in another direction and cultivate radical individualism. It isn't a matter of loving ourselves more than other people; rather, we are too preoccupied with ourselves to have much time for others. Although we yearn for other people and may love them dearly, we just can't let them get too close.

Midlife is a watershed of adult development, a time when the illusion of individual autonomy gives way to recognition of dependence on others. Instead of fighting against the wider aspect of ourselves, we can now adopt a yielding posture toward nature. This means accepting our bond to family and reaching out to friends. But close relationships with family and friends are not all there is to the wider self.

The Creative Potential of Work

Many of the heroes of Gail Sheehy's *Passages* and *Pathfinders* find happiness in midlife by renouncing the quest for success and settling down to enjoy their families. (Although this may become a problem for women in the future, it is still pretty much a man's issue.) Daniel Levinson describes a similar switch from career to family values as part of male maturation. Doing so is easier, as Levinson recognizes, after a man has achieved some measure of success. Paul E. Tsongas announced his resignation from the U.S. Senate to resume his law practice and spend more time with his family. Originally he gave health as the reason, but later revealed that he had "sacrificed his family for his career" and now wanted to redress the balance. A lot of people cheer at this kind of announcement.

The trouble with these stories is that they portray family and career as incompatible commitments, competing for the mature adult's time. The result is the appearance of a false choice: either devote yourself to work or change priorities and put the family first. A full life is balanced, with multiple sources of satisfaction, providing breadth and insuring flexibility. A mature adult's context begins with, but does not end with, family. It also includes the extended family, friends, and a vocation. I say "vocation" not because I got tired of writing "career," but in order to recognize that a person may find fulfillment and give service in ways other than working for a paycheck.

So many working people are unhappy because work is only a means to an end. They don't find pleasure in it and they don't take pride in it. They do it only to get somewhere—but some never arrive. Studs Terkel's book *Working* is filled with stories of working men and women who are miserable. It doesn't seem to matter whether they are laborers or high-powered professionals; most people don't like what they do. A typical example of what Terkel found when he interviewed people about their work was a thirty-seven-year-old steelworker. He hates his work. He's tired. He thinks what he does is meaningless, because nothing he does leaves any personal signature. He feels no pride because there is nothing he can point to and say, "I made that." So he's resigned. But he hopes for more for his children.

"If you can't improve yourself, you improve your posterity. Otherwise life isn't worth living." Unfortunately, he's too busy working to get to know his children.

Even the upscale workaholic professional, driven to succeed, may not enjoy work. If people don't derive pleasure from work, if work is only a means to an end, then they are in for a big letdown when they realize that they aren't going to be rich and famous. That letdown is one of the root causes of the midlife crisis.

The hours from nine to five are too long to spend in an occupation that is not satisfying in its own right. But here is where a lot of people bump up against hard reality. It's all very well to write about the experiential value of work, but what about all the people (most of us) hemmed in by financial need on one side and limited mobility on the other?

There are two useful strategies for achieving balanced satisfaction from work: putting work in perspective and making the hours at work pay off. Some people *do* place too high a priority on their jobs, seeking from work more than it can provide. If the only way one gets any satisfaction is chasing achievement, one gets pretty lonely. The solution is not to cease striving, but to stop the self-defeating total dominance of career aspirations. This is indicated especially for those people who work, not for the satisfaction it provides, but only as a means to an end.

The second strategy is to create a work situation that *is* satisfying. Some people accomplish this only by making a career switch. Many jobs *are* oppressive and draining. Sometimes the job we have doesn't really suit us; we took it because it paid well, offered security, or was dictated by loyalty to some family script. Sometimes a job meets our needs at one stage of life, but later our needs change or we move up to a role which doesn't suit us (the "Peter Principle"). Seniority and security may keep us stuck. Realizing what's at stake—the heart of your days for the next twenty years—gives some people the courage to risk making a change. Other people find vocational meaning and purpose by reorganizing what they are already doing.

Before you decide to leave a job, be as clear as possible about where the problem lies. Are the limitations you feel primarily imposed by the job, or is your rut of your own making? If the limits are in the situation, try pushing those limits. If they don't move, maybe you should. If you decide to leave, don't do so precipitously. Enlist the support of friends and give yourself a safety net. If possible take a leave of absence to explore the new job. That way you have the option to return if the new job doesn't work out.

Of the people I know who have made constructive changes in midlife, a few have cut back on exaggerated commitments to careers. Larger by far, though, are the number of people who faced up to the fact that they didn't like what they were doing and made career changes. Two people left prestigious academic institutions for smaller schools, where they would have more autonomy. Two people quit working for large companies and went into business for themselves. One person recognized that he had always placed too high a priority on work, seeking success and acclaim to compensate for a basic feeling of insecurity. His solution was not the obvious. Along with the realization that career success would never give full meaning and satisfaction to his life, he also decided that he could reach a slightly higher plateau by working harder! He did so, putting in extra hours and weekends for a year or so, achieving some of the fame that he had sought, and then cutting back and spending more time with his family.

9

The Psychotherapeutic Solution

CONDITIONED by a culture of specialization, Americans turn with increasing frequency to experts to solve their problems. We now have specialists to attend to every aspect of health and well-being. No matter what ails us in midlife, somewhere there is a specialist to turn to. We have chiropractors, osteopaths, and neuropaths; heart surgeons and cosmetic surgeons; specialists in internal medicine and physical medicine, sports medicine and psychosomatic medicine; and on and on.

When we suffer sickness of the spirit, we seek out doctors of the soul. In earlier, more spiritual times, this was likely to be a minister of religion. In the 1980s, it is more likely to be a "minister" of psychotherapy, the secular priests of our times.

Psychotherapeutic salvation, like older forms, implies giving over personal responsibility to a sanctified authority, a higher power. Plagued by anxiety, depression, and a sense of inner emptiness, people turn to psychotherapy for "mental health," the modern equivalent of redemption. (It's interesting to note that as psychotherapists displace preachers, preachers, priests, and rabbis are getting into psychotherapy, in the guise of "pastoral counseling.") What makes psychiatric explanations even more attractive is that they tend to absolve the individual of responsibility. To say that people fail to find meaning in life or form close attachments because of fragile egos is to imply that they cannot help it. If we cannot help what we are, it seems to follow that we cannot change. We are victims. By extension this logic leads to a vastly inflated opinion of how much change is possible in psychotherapy.

Clinicians and patients alike contribute to the overvaluation of psychological healing. Psychotherapy, as it began with Freud, was a specialized form of treatment for a specific small group of patients, hysterical neurotics. Since that time it has evolved into a growth industry. Today this industry may be oversold, a victim of its own success. Psychology has an explanation—and a cure—for every problem. Even professional football teams now have their own "sports psychologists." Experts accept the status that this dependence conveys on them and respond with a superabundance of conflicting advice.

Why are so many people so eager to turn over their problems to psychotherapists? Most people do not give in easily to dependence. Even so, we long to. Lurking beneath our independent attitude is a passion for authority. We long for dependency but fear closeness. The average person can have the former without an undue amount of the latter in psychotherapy.

Conditioned by the medical model to place blind trust in the practitioner, many people bring themselves to psychotherapy as they might bring their cars in for repair: "Here's the problem; fix it." A more useful model might be the educational one. Just as in education, where learning is a process of interaction, so in psychotherapy, therapists can only teach if the patient wants to learn. And, as there is little learning without homework, there is no analysis without self-reflection. Whether a therapist dispenses advice or analysis, the end result depends on the patient. Interpretations do not create insight and change; they are only the impetus for setting in motion processes of self-scrutiny. But most people are slow to accept this.

By the time they ask for help many people have given up on themselves and are ready for an expert to take over. What do they seek? Comfort? Always. Counsel? Sometimes. Change? Rarely, and reluctantly. We might like the idea of change, but we want someone to change us (or change the person who seems to be causing our problems).

A thirty-nine-year-old woman came to consult me about her marriage. She had been married for sixteen years. Her husband, a failed entrepreneur, treated her badly from the start; the only interest she had in him was trying to push him into succeeding with one of his many ventures. Early in the marriage she realized that it was a mistake, but she hoped that things would change in time. They didn't. She tried psychotherapy once or twice, but that didn't work either. Now she knows that she should leave him, but doesn't want to go through the unpleasantness of a separation and divorce. At this point I asked, "So, you'd like my help?" "Oh, yes!" "You'd like to leave your husband, but avoid all the unpleasantness and turmoil?" "Yes!" "It can't be done." She went away, presumably to find a psychotherapist who would be more "understanding."

A model that appeals to many people is that of hypnotism (not the real hypnotism, but a psychological sorcery that is a product of our own wishful thinking). Suppose you could lose ten pounds, quit smoking, stop worrying, make friends more easily, or overcome your irritability simply by slipping into a deep trance. People have a longing to be hypnotized, not only because they want the illusion of change without paying the price, but also because they want to get back to a magically protective relationship. This is particularly true of those people who enter midlife with unfulfilled needs for attention and praise. When these needs are intense and when we fail to find the echo of understanding acceptance, they arouse feelings of shame and emptiness. The empty self suppresses those needs and compensates either by trying to fill up the emptiness with accomplishment, or by self-sacrifice to the needs of others, or by withdrawing altogether from intimate relations. People shun intimacy, not because they are disinterested, but because their need is so intense it frightens them.

The empty self longs for an idealized parent figure, someone to borrow strength from. Psychotherapists appear to lack the uncertainty and self-doubts that bedevil the rest of us. Most of us are partly blind to and partly unable to change the habits of a lifetime. Instead, bent on improving our lot, we cast about until we find an expert who offers a truth that will set us free. We follow the plan and at first achieve some change. But if the therapist's plan is not our plan, deep changes are slow in coming. At this point, people either drop out or follow with a dishonest heart.

Psychotherapists, like hypnotists, achieve their most cherished effects by tapping into ordinary processes. They don't create anything new; they just bring out latent human possibilities. No matter what terms the experts use, the payoff is developing interpersonal competence. Demystifying the institution of psychotherapy robs it of some of its magical appeal, but seeing it for what it is may make it possible to use it for what it can do. The "it," psychotherapy, is not just an institution, but a relationship. It isn't "psychotherapy" that works or not; it is the relationship, how we approach it and how we deal with it.

Psychotherapy seems to offer a way to break the bounds of human nature. But there is no way to transcend the limits of the human condition. This is not to say that psychotherapy cannot give great gifts to tortured and overwhelmed people and greater connectedness to those who value and can use it. What can we hope for? New adaptations, creative solutions to our problems, and greater openness to other people. Psychotherapy can help lift the load of neurotic guilt, enabling us to unblock bottled-up passion and embrace the nature of the real world. Psychotherapy can also help affirm our selves as centers of initiative and value. This strengthening of the self, in turn, allows us to embrace other people more openly; we are able to stand closer together because we are able to stand alone.

Finding the Right Therapy

"When should I go to therapy?" This is a logical question that not many people ask.

The decision is usually determined by the push and pull of motives that aren't consciously deliberated. The choice is predicated on the lack of resistance and the push of hurt. Resistance involves practical considerations, such as expense and the availability of competent therapists. It's also attitudinal; some people don't like to ask for help, don't want to examine their own lives, or don't trust experts. Where resistance is low, minimal distress may be sufficient motivation. Frequent clients of psychotherapy are therapists, who naturally accept the psychotherapeutic solution to problems, and people who work for large employers, *par excellence* the government, because insurance benefits reduce the expense to a minimum. At the other extreme are those who, despite the burden of expense and their own reluctance, seek therapy because of severe problems. Recently, in my own practice I saw a couple with only a slight problem in communication; their treatment was paid in full by a prepaid health plan. In the same week I saw a woman who waited until her despair reached a suicidal extreme before asking for help; she could afford the expense but was a strong believer in solving her own problems.

In deciding whether to consult a psychotherapist, you might want to consider whether you are unable to make changes on your own or whether you simply haven't tried. If you have worked on your problems but can't seem to make headway, perhaps you could profit from professional help. With difficult relationships, have you tried to work them out directly with the person involved, or do you shrink away? The chronicity of the problem is a relevant, though not determining, consideration. If the problem has persisted for a long time, then it is more likely to be something you are doing, rather than something that is happening to you. Still, even where difficulty has persisted for years, don't expect the therapeutic relationship to do away with the problems. Whatever problems you have in life, you will bring with you to psychotherapy. If you are lucky, the therapist will point this out, but don't count on it.

"How do I chose a therapist?" This is a more practical and frequently asked question.

The current scene is a jumble of conflicting schools, each with its own jargon and its own version of truth. There is psychodynamic therapy, client-centered therapy, existential therapy, humanistic therapy, gestalt therapy, cognitive therapy, rational emotive therapy, family therapy, group therapy, psychosynthesis, primal therapy, reality therapy, biofeedback, behavior therapy, transactional analysis, megavitamin therapy, hypnosis, etcetera, etcetera. Even among psychoanalysts, there are Freudians, Jungians, Adlerians, Reichians, Sullivanians, Kleinians, and Kohutians. To further confuse the issue, some practitioners advertise according to what they treat without specifying what they do. For example, there are phobia clinics (usually behavioral), depression clinics (usually testing a new medication), eating disorders clinics (usually a combination of psychodynamics and behavior modification), single parent groups (usually self-help), stress management groups (usually cognitive or behavioral), and so on. Many therapists don't like to be pigeonholed—some because they are eclectic, and others because they don't wish to limit their clientele to those who are sympathetic to their particular brand of therapy—and so patients may have to find out the hard way, by costly and time-consuming trial and error. You can minimize the confusion and aggravation by selecting a therapist, not a method. Look for the best therapist available; ask several people who may be in a position to know—friends who have benefited from psychotherapy, wise physicians, or the faculty of nearby medical or graduate schools. Note names that are recommended more than once.

In the 1960s the new therapies of the human potential movement called for a kind of self-fulfillment that was inherently narcissistic, narrowly self-centered, and hedonistic. "Do your own thing" and "let it all hang out" were the catchphrases. In the process, followers were sometimes led to neglect their families, undermining not only duty and obligation but also the fulfillment of their larger self-interest. The human potential movement called for open feeling, self-expression, and love—but often divorced these sentiments from the family. The love that bloomed in the hothouse climate of an encounter weekend usually dried up on Monday.

Since the sixties, psychotherapists have followed the culture into more sober times. Today there is a reemergence of depth psychotherapy, in which people are urged to come to terms with their inner selves and the legacy of their early family lives. At the same time, family therapy has gained enormous popularity by dealing with the residue of these early experiences as it is played out in the contemporary family.

Individual psychotherapy and family therapy—we have seen how these two approaches to human experience offer explanations for the problems of adults in midlife. Which is better for you? The dimensions—self and others—are linked together; you can approach change from the inside out or the outside in. Either way, progress is circular.

However decided, the choice of therapy is influenced by context and economics. People who can afford private psychotherapy are apt to see either psychodynamic or humanistic practitioners; people who cannot afford private psychotherapy are likely to go to clinics, where they are more apt to be treated with behavior therapy or family therapy. When people make conscious choices about which approach to select, they are often shoring up already overdeveloped aspects of their personalities. Obsessional thinkers want to understand everything and therefore gravitate to psychoanalytic therapy; people who want quick solutions without really examining or changing themselves may opt for behavior therapy.

Prospective patients should bear in mind that their midlife crisis is like a Rorschach test for the therapist, calling forth hidden reverberations to his or her own frustrated dreams. If a couple is in danger of breaking up, what fantasies does this call forth in the therapist? To some it may conjure up the exciting possibility of freedom and gratification; to others it may mean the threat of abandonment and emptiness. All therapists espouse neutrality, but what do they really think? and feel? and say? Professional experts are capable of undermining our freedom to choose, but only if we let them.

Therapists have a tendency to push people in certain directions. Some announce it by their affiliation (if you can read the clues). "Marriage counselors," for example, generally strive to keep the family together, rather than limiting themselves to helping resolve conflicts. "Women's therapists" tend to politicize personal problems, and some may encourage women to think of their husbands and other males as oppressors. "Humanistic" therapists are champions of individuality, risk-taking, and emotional expression; they are likely to question duty and obligation. I have already suggested that if you want to try psychotherapy, look around for the most highly recommended therapist in town. But the process of change does not begin and end at the door of the consulting room.

An Expensive Friendship

People enter psychotherapy hoping to repair problems in living. Too often what they get is a form of conversion and substitute gratification. When patients trade in their own goals (reducing anxiety, say, or overcoming loneliness) for the therapist's (analytic insight or emotional ventilation), they cease to be patients and become disciples. The problem with this is that disciples come away with a guru or a master without whom they are lost and cannot function. Sometimes the guru offers friendship.

In *Psychotherapy: The Purchase of Friendship*, William Schofield noted that many people have as their closest friend someone they see only once a week and whom they have to pay to talk to. Life then centers on the weekly hour of therapy. As long as this ritual experience serves as the center of meaning and the only moving relationship, psychotherapy becomes an expensive substitute for, rather than preparation for, life itself. How can this happen, and why?

The psychotherapeutic relationship provides reliable shelter for deep yearnings for emotional safety, in which the authentic self can emerge. I am impressed by the number of men and women in midlife who begin therapy with a painful confession. Most of the time, these "confessions" involve ordinary human emotions that took on frightening proportions because they were held beneath the surface for years. These confessions often remind me of guilt-ridden adolescents and their revelations about masturbation. While the confessions of midlife may not be as naïve, many people torture themselves for years about relatively common human feelings.

Sometimes a man who enjoys looking at other men's bodies fears that he may be "constitutionally" homosexual. Sometimes a woman says she secretly hates her children or perhaps fantasizes about other men when she is with her husband or lover. Most revelations are not specific secrets, but fears and longings that are denied expression. Disturbances of narcissistic balance are recognized by the embarrassment and shame that the person feels. These defects in self-esteem determine what is sought in the therapeutic relationship. The weak and empty self relates to others as "self-objects"—that is, as parent figures who either respond to and confirm goodness and worth or become images of strength: mirror and merger. In life these needs are subdued; in therapy they are reactivated.

In fact, therapy is a good place to become aware of unmet needs and come to terms with them, but they must be seen rather than acted out. And then they must be integrated into everyday relationships. The ideal of analysis is a good one. The analyst does not offer friendship and does not return it. Instead, he or she holds the patient's motivation up for examination. But a therapist's official orientation is a less sure guarantee than his or her personal perspective on life. Mature therapists do not need their patients as friends. Still, as patients, we must be aware of the difference between feeling in therapy and making changes in life. Healing is a sham if it depends on the continued presence of the therapist or if therapy displaces natural relationships.

The award-winning film *Ordinary People* illustrated the paradoxical effects of triangulation. The story involved a family of three, husband Calvin and wife Beth, who had a conflicted and distant relationship, and Conrad, the seventeen-year-old son who was depressed and guilty after his older brother's death in a boating accident. While seeming to present a balanced and realistic portrayal of a modern family in trouble, the film contained one villain—a cold and distant mother—and one hero—a sensitive and compassionate therapist. While the parents tried unsuccessfully to resolve their marital conflict, the son became suicidally depressed. Fortunately, the son was cured; unfortunately, the parents split up. One thing that audiences felt most strongly in this immensely popular film was how lucky the boy was to find a therapist who provided the missing parental understanding. Overlooked was the fact that while the patient was cured, the family died. Here was a family where a woman, feeling unloved by her husband, was unable to offer her son the nurturance he needed to help him overcome the terrible loss of his brother. The therapist, in this maternal role, served as a third leg on the triangle between mother and son, enabling the son to find help while perpetuating his alienation from his mother. Had the whole family gone to therapy together the outcome might have been the same, but at least the therapist would have had the opportunity to heal the patient without taking him out of his natural context.

Although the various schools of individual therapy have conceptual disagreements with one another, they share a number of unquestioned basic assumptions. Freudians and self psychologists, for example, may disagree whether repressed drives or fragile self-esteem are the root cause of adult unhappiness, but they never doubt that the primary forces shaping and maintaining behavior are located within the individual. Individual therapists recognize the importance of family life in shaping the personality, but assume that these forces are internalized and that interior personality dynamics become the dominant forces that determine behavior. Treatment, therefore, can and should be directed at the person and his or her personal makeup. Family therapists, on the other hand, acknowledge that past experiences are encoded in individuals, but consider these influences to be weaker than current interpersonal interactions. Treatment, from the family perspective, is most powerful and effective when it is applied directly to the organization of the family.

The Family Therapy Alternative

The family therapy alternative works by bringing people together in order to transform their interactions. The focus of treatment may be a family, an unmarried couple, or even a work group. Most people who consider psychotherapy when they are unhappy think first of individual therapy. The last thing most of us want is to bring along those people we have trouble with. The danger of yielding to this reluctance is the danger of avoiding confronting problems at their source. The great advantage of family therapy is that it works directly with the unhappy human relationships that propel most people into therapy.

A neighbor once asked me at a party, "Does family therapy really work?" It was one of those questions that catches a person off-guard; I was reminded of "The Emperor's New Clothes." What I said was that a third of the time people come during a crisis and the crisis passes almost no matter what they do; a third of the time going to a therapist's office is a way to start talking and the process of talking itself often helps; and perhaps a third of the time a family is really stuck with a problem and is fortunate enough to find a therapist who helps them make some significant changes and then lets go. As in individual therapy, the outcome depends on a willingness to examine one's own role.

Because it does not involve a retreat from troubled and troubling relationships, family therapy is less likely than individual therapy to become a substitute form of dependency, but even in family therapy the universal longing to turn one's problems over to experts may come into play. One of the potential problems with family therapy is that some therapists take over when there is a missing role or function in the family, the therapist takes over. This means that things are okay only as long as the therapy continues. Therapists do this when they give specific advice for every problem that comes up or act as referees rather than facilitators. Unhappy clients let therapists take over when they see therapy as a place to solve their problems, rather than as a place to learn how to solve them themselves. A couple of friends of mine once started to have an argument. It seemed like an ordinary dispute; what was interesting was that they seemed to have a covert agreement to avoid finishing the discussion. I was puzzled, because I knew they could easily have settled it. Later, when I asked, both said they were postponing the discussion until their weekly couples therapy session. They were saving the argument for their therapist, like a present.

An alternative problem can arise if therapists intervene without increasing people's ability to solve their own problems. Once again, however, what we get out of therapy is what we take out of therapy. If the therapist is not a good teacher, then we must try harder to be good learners.

Family therapy may be the treatment of choice when pressing problems revolve around the children. Their personalities are still so malleable that the greatest benefit can often be achieved by influencing their family environment. Adults are also embedded in the family, but life in the family is organized by ingrained habits encoded in the psyches of its members. Neither influence is independent. Readjustments can often be made by simply tuning up current interactions. Definitive change, however, is less likely without overhauling ingrained modes of experience. This experience is available in family therapy, but not if the participants reduce human action to the surface of behavior. Efforts to "improve communication" don't get far when inner fears of closeness block liberating dialogue.

There's another problem with family therapy: with the whole system present, it is easy for each family member to project responsibility for change onto the others. In individual therapy it is clear who must change, but when the responsibility is diffused throughout the group, family members often wait for someone else to go first. The fate of the family is determined by active human agency, not by some abstract, occult "family dynamics." A couple's pattern of criticism and avoidance may be "circular" and "homeostatic," but it is perpetuated by individual actions. Family dynamics mean that actions of the individual are influenced in unseen ways by the actions of others—*not* that individual action doesn't matter. By suggesting that families run according to laws of their own, family systems theorists reveal a truth but create a mystifying effect on the role of the individual. The only person you can change is yourself.

Taking Charge of Change

In everyday life, we maintain limits on self-awareness by running away whenever anxiety exceeds a certain level. When we are alone, thinking about our lives, we are usually careful not to get too close to certain painful conclusions. When we are with others, if conversation gets too hot, we may change the subject or walk away. In therapy we can't walk away because the door is closed, at least for three-quarters of an hour, once a week. This structured confinement makes it possible to extend the limits of self-examination; it also mobilizes anxiety and resistance.

"Resistance," meaning forces within the patient that oppose the progress of treatment, is one of the primary concerns of all psychotherapists. Patients resist psychotherapy more or less automatically, because we all tend to cling to familiar modes of experience and to defend ourselves against probes that threaten our defenses. It is a natural expression of our humanity to hold on to our personal view of things. As individuals we create filters of meaning from which to organize our experience, and as natural groups we prefer familiar patterns of relating to the unknown. Therapy works by helping us expand the range of our choices, but that is precisely why it is so difficult.

The usual view of resistance pits the therapist as an opponent of a negative force within the patient, making therapy a battle that depends upon the power of the therapist. If, instead, we are to assume responsibility for our own changing (in therapy or out) we must not depend on someone else to make it happen. In resistance, patients encounter the fear of breaking out, focused on some crucial process in psychotherapy. The rigidly overcontrolled person may not allow himself or herself to free associate, thereby stalemating the therapist's attempts to find out what the person is afraid might come out. The timid and anxious person may do everything that is required in therapy, except the one crucial thing: telling the therapist about his or her feelings. Human nature, with its powerful defensive trend, leads us in the direction of least resistance. But we do not have to follow.

Our responsibility for our own lives never ceases; therapists don't change us, and we must work hard to profit from therapy. This may mean sticking with it when sessions are painful or remembering what we'd like to forget. Taking responsibility for getting the most out of therapy involves a paradox. Once you carefully choose a therapist, put yourself in his or her hands. Don't fight the method. Take what there is to get from the experience. If your therapist is a Freudian, learn what there is to learn about how you defend against expressing your drives. If the therapist is an emotivist, learn to overcome barriers to full feeling. In any form of therapy, patients are likely to be aware of what the therapist is doing—and not doing. My advice is to accept these limits and concentrate on profiting from what the therapist does offer. Therapists can only teach if patients are willing to learn.

In the final analysis, change is an intensely personal project. Therapy is not a panacea for human problems. No external agency can take us out of our predicament and guarantee creative living. We need private initiative and personal responsibility. Ironically, the very institution dedicated to increasing human freedom seems to deny the possibility of personal freedom. Since Freud, there has been a decisive shift from the simplistic and moralistic belief that behavior is entirely under conscious control to the idea that the person is ruled by inaccessible, unconscious forces. But the fact that choices are constrained does not mean that choice is eliminated.

Psychotherapy is not the only route to change. Religion, a

new friendship, in fact any positive relationship in the natural environment may have a therapeutic impact. A therapeutic relationship is one in which we feel safe enough to take a look at ourselves. Unfortunately, in a social climate where concern, tenderness, and wisdom are rare, such circumstances are difficult to find.

Entering therapy is a decision to stop running away from our inner selves and our families. Therapists can help us to stand still and to endure the anxiety that comes from facing our personal demons. They cannot give us courage, but they can give acceptance and affirmation. Therapy is a two-stage process —first comes understanding, then change. It takes tact and genuine warmth to coax the shy self into the open. Patients are most apt to respond with rage and resistance, not because they are threatened with change, but because they feel their selves —that is, their integrity—being attacked. Sensitive clinicians know this intuitively and teach with gentleness born of respect. Self-directed change is no different. Whether you choose therapy or not, you will have to work at change. But the work must begin with acceptance.

To have it all, we must discover the "all" that is available, satisfying, and real. Grace requires no extraordinary action; it requires living in the ordinary world with open acceptance of what is. Life can be arbitrary and unfair. We have no control over that. What we do have control over is how we respond.

10

Finding Yourself at Forty

HOWEVER the midlife crisis is first manifest, the solution is to discover who you really are and what you really want. We've seen that "finding yourself" becomes a preoccupation for many people in midlife. But what does finding yourself mean?

As a nondirective psychotherapist I am skeptical of universal solutions. Giving advice is like leading a horse to water; what happens next is up to the horse. Advice doesn't work when it is passively received. Something stronger has to happen, something that transforms a person's attitudes or way of perceiving. In times of crisis, life itself serves up the "something stronger."

What must we do to expand rather than diminish the promise of our lives? Before we move forward, we need to know where we are. Begin by trying to get a better idea of who you are as a person. Examine your life and your experience. Don't rush this evaluation. Take your time; but ask yourself: What is your life like? Where will you be ten years from now? What would you like to be doing? What do you like about yourself?

Dislike? Do you enjoy your work? What about your family? Have you made a place in your life for friendship? If you feel unloved, are you willing to be the author of feeling unloved? Are you willing to switch the responsibility from "out there" to "in here"? Are you willing to be the cause of your life, or are you stuck being the effect?

Experience Delivers

T. S. Eliot once asked, "Where is the life we lose by living?" How is it possible to lose life by living? The answer lies in how we live it. Life slides by when we focus more on the future than on the present. Anticipation serves to keep us going, but experience delivers.

We cultivate the discipline of delay in order to get ahead. We work long hours to put the kids through school, take classes at night to upgrade our skills, and sweat hard to stay in shape. Over the years this orientation to the future pays off. Better students get better jobs, harder workers get promotions. But some people overdo it. Practice becomes habit. Those of us who dutifully keep our noses to the grindstone have been told, "You ought to relax more; take it easy; have some fun." Once we thought that kind of advice frivolous, out of touch with our serious purpose. By midlife, we begin to realize that life is now, not somewhere in the future.

We act within the limits of what we know and see and feel, and when this takes us as far as it can, we may look to others to suggest new courses of action. The trouble with action remedies is they suggest that life is a struggle and we must be combatants. As long as life is seen as a problem to solve, it makes sense to see only what we need to in order to get on with our quest. In the morning, for example, we keep our eyes fixed on the road to work—never mind the trees and human faces along the way. This same tunnel vision keeps us operating within fixed images of ourselves and other people. It isn't action that's needed but expanding the limits within which we operate.

In youth, we were in touch with the living tip of life, where there were dangers, temptations, and hurts, as well as the full pleasure of sensation. We got wet when it rained, sometimes our noses got bloodied, and often our feelings were stung. So we learned to protect ourselves, to insulate ourselves from the elements. We, who once lived with all kinds of weather, have grown used to air-conditioned summers and electrically heated winters. The same thing can happen to our hearts. If we smother emotion and desire to avoid conflict and risk, we end up in a climate of emotional deadness.

The Perceptive Center

Renewal begins with understanding; understanding begins with awareness. The simplest kind of awareness—sensation and perception—may seem banal, but it is central to everything else. By this I mean coming to our senses—rediscovering the physical and the present tense. At the heart of human experience is the perceptive center. Etymology recognizes this; the derivations of some of our most cherished values come from sensate experience: from "senses" we get sensitive. To be sensitive you must engage your senses. From "see" we get insight and visionary. From "touch" we get "to be touched" —to feel deeply and to allow ourselves to let experience penetrate. To "hear" we must listen. How many of us really listen, really hear, when others are talking to us? Or are we usually half-listening, while preparing our own response? Only by listening can we let people in; otherwise we are "impenetrable." From "taste" comes the idea of savoring. Savoring the tastes and smells of life all around stimulates interest and zest. To relish life is to dwell on experience with delight.

Cherishing your sensibilities is not the same as hectic seeking of sensation. It doesn't mean traveling to exotic places or courting expensive pleasures; it means living the life that's all around you. It may mean slowing down and relaxing into what you are already doing; it may mean rediscovering play. Pay attention; allow yourself to be moved by new experience. Try this little exercise. From time to time, spend five minutes just looking at some object. It needn't be something unique or compelling; the idea is to concentrate on what is at hand, not to be captivated. Don't think, don't plan, don't move; just look. At first you may find it hard to do this for as long as one minute. Keep practicing. This little trick is a form of meditation, but it is designed to help you tune in rather than tune out.

One person I spoke to said that she sees things more freshly simply by sitting down with a cup of coffee in an unfamiliar room or a far corner of the backyard. Another person takes five minutes once in a while to write down every sound he hears. Doing so, he says, helps him break routine patterns of experience and makes him more aware of what's going on.

Turn off the radio in the car; go for a walk in a new part of town; sit on a bench and just think. Some people find that keeping a journal helps; others write down their dreams or talk things over with friends. Let your awareness incubate.

One of the great appeals of painting (or visiting art galleries) is not so much creating a product, but training the eye to see. A game I sometimes play is to close my eyes for a few moments while I'm walking. When I open them I see my surroundings much more vividly. Poetry is another art form well suited to discovery, because the poet creates meaning and value from ordinary experience.

Poetry? When we come home at night many of us are too worn out for anything more challenging than television or a drink. At least that's true for me. But here are a couple of tips I've found useful. If you want to start stretching your imagination, find a time when you do have some energy. For some people this means early morning; for others it means late at night or on weekends. Think of yourself as expanding your experience in small steps. If you have lost the habit of reading good literature, for example, it might be better not to start with Proust or some other weighty tome you think you "should" read. Try something that may be a little easier to get into. Don't set yourself up for failure.

You may discover as you change your attitude that you want to change more than that. Not just the big things. Most people's lives are filled with activities that numb the spirit and drain vital energy. Often it's the little things, things we hardly notice, that get us down.

Midlife is still filled with obligations and imperatives. Most of us have to keep working whether we like it or not, and taking out the garbage is necessary, even if not inspiring. Even if 90 percent of our time is taken up with commitments we choose to honor, that still leaves a good many activities that are optional. They *are* optional even though we may not perceive them that way. We don't have to answer the phone every time it rings, drive the kids wherever they want to go, attend all the PTA meetings, mow the lawn every Saturday, work late whenever we are asked, watch the news every night, keep the house spotless, automatically say yes when asked to do a favor, accept invitations from people who don't particularly interest us, go to all of those office parties, etcetera, etcetera. Upon reflection, we may want to continue doing many of these things, but probably not all.

Think of all the things *you already know about* that energize and enrich you. Often these require extra effort or for some reason are easy to let slip away. If you were to list in one column your ten favorite activities and then note in a parallel column the last time you did them, you would probably realize how much you have given up. With so much of life taken up by what we have to do, we ought to be pretty choosy about the things we volunteer to do. Spend a week taking inventory of the optional activities in your life; notice which activities are numbing, which not.

Action or Insight?

Creative change involves action and insight. Sometimes one achieves a significant breakthrough in only one of these dimensions—for example, the woman who forces herself to go to Parents without Partners despite her shyness or the man who suddenly realizes that he must make time for friends. Sustained and lasting change, however, is likely to require both action and insight. By learning more about who we are—what we want and what we are afraid of—we can *then* expand the bounds of our experience. The process is like the child's game of leapfrog: awareness, action, awareness.

Insight is often regarded as a magical solution, the great "aha" that unlocks all doors. This notion is misleading. Deeper understanding comes from reflecting on the experience of two kinds of action: automatic action avoided, and avoided action overcome. Not everyone withdraws in the face of criticism or seeks distraction from sadness, but each of us has a personal version of running away from feelings. Most of us also have a variety of rituals that help us to avoid certain feelings in the first place. For example, some people always come late to meetings to avoid the anxiety of unstructured chatting; some people tell themselves that they don't have time for fun because they have more important things to do. You can discover some of these neurotic habits by considering the things you do excessively (or compulsively). These are the ones that make you anxious if you don't do them. You can learn a lot about yourself by standing still in the face of anxiety. I don't mean masochistic resignation to unpleasant experience, but a resolute commitment to facing your feelings, neither smothering them, distracting yourself, or acting them out precipitously. To be alive is to feel intensely, sharply, variously. Feel your feelings, and then think about their implications.

The second type of action is experimenting with new situations or those you usually avoid. Open yourself to novelty. Many of us follow an unspoken rule that says that we don't do something for fun unless we feel like it. The unfortunate result is a vicious circle of not-feeling-like and not-doing. For one week, try a couple of the following (whether you feel like it or not): go for a walk at dawn, take a swim at lunchtime, call a friend you haven't spoken to in years, take someone out to breakfast during the workweek, visit a place in your town where "only tourists go"; choose something that contrasts with how you usually spend your time.

If you are sedentary, do something active; if you are a private person, do something social. The purpose of these experiments is not necessarily to pick something inherently rewarding, but more to understand what it feels like to do certain things you don't often do. If you haven't given a party lately or spent some time alone or struck up a conversation with a stranger, then try it. The first time you put yourself in an unfamiliar situation you may feel uncomfortable. The point is to learn more about yourself by expanding your sphere of activity.

Lifting Repression

We can achieve fuller life by overcoming habits of repression. In the conflict between the ego, the id, and reality, something has to give. In neurosis the ego accepts reality (unquestioned) and turns its energy against the id. The normal human neurosis that most of us suffer from consists of surplus repression that uses up energy, which explains why the repressed person feels tired much of the time. When midlife adults think about running away and starting over (the Gauguin fantasy), they are declaring war on reality. The healthier course is to reexamine reality. We maintain repression because of our exaggerated fears of repressed impulses and their imagined dangerous consequences. We are like the ancients who populated unknown oceans with imaginary sea monsters. But is the world around us really as restrictive as we think?

Lifting repression may be difficult, but we can start by dismantling some of the outer structures of defense. Often our defenses are encoded in relationships with others. Most of us are surrounded by people we elect to deprive us of pleasure: the bosses who hold us back, keeping us from the rewards of success; the women (or men) who torture us by restricting our fun; the men (or women) who rob us of initiative and responsibility. Frequently, the strongest control seems to be exerted over us by family members.

When we think of others as controlling us and denying us pleasure, we are, to a large extent, projecting our own repressions. In tricking ourselves to look outside rather than in, we avoid the unsettling recognition of past conflicts, but also neglect the opportunity to resolve them. Instead of projecting blame, it may be more useful to contemplate why we may be conflicted over expressing our wishes. What would happen if we did what "they won't let us do"? Self-pitying rationalization stands, or rather falls, with the idea that we are children in a world of grownups. When and how might we have learned to fear the consequences of arguing, indulging ourselves, traveling alone, opening up to strangers, or sitting around doing nothing?

A thirty-eight-year-old woman who felt trapped in a life without any fun to it assumed that the problem was her marriage. "I thought that being free meant being single. But then I considered what I would do if I were free, and realized that maybe I could just start doing some of those things. I began going out with my women friends more often, took the train to the city for a weekend of shopping, and I started reading in the evening while my husband watched TV. It took my husband a little while to get used to my doing more things for myself, but he didn't raise nearly as much of a fuss as I expected."

Consider some of the things you'd like to do but *can't*. "I'd love to have more free time . . . sit around and do nothing all weekend . . . spend more time with the kids . . . go camping . . . take a winter vacation in the sun." Some of these wishes have costs you may not be willing to assume. Taking a winter vacation in the islands means making a number of complicated arrangements and spending a lot of money, neither of which you may want to do. Actually taking the vacation (or going camping) may be less important than daydreaming about it and feeling deprived. When we think about being deprived, it's common to blame someone—we can't because "they won't let us." For instance, "I wish I could have a drink after work with my friends, but my wife wouldn't understand." Blaming is even more likely when chores we "have to" do begin to bore us. "I used to like to cook, but I hate to have to fix dinner every night. Unfortunately, my husband expects it."

Make no mistake: if you begin to change, your imaginary

jailors may truly act the way you fear they will. The boss may yell at you for your more relaxed hours; your husband probably will complain if meals are more haphazard, or initially oppose your going away for the weekend. Your wife may very well get annoyed if you change your habits, if you start expressing your anger, or become more passionate. What is less likely, however, is that their doing so will be the disaster you imagine.

We encounter the nay-saying superego whenever we depart from old (approved) ways. Even if "they" don't say anything we may feel uncomfortable with new behavior. One way to start breaking this habit of self-imposed restraint is to review all the things that our parents (authors of our superegos) taught us about what we "should" do and what we "shouldn't" do. We can then discover the power to negate irrational fears.

In truth, letting the self out of its cocoon is hazardous—we *do* encounter conflict when we expand the range of our activities. As the unrealized promises of the self are disinterred, so too are its tender spots. But in the process of seeing and feeling, we rediscover what is unique and idiosyncratic, and begin to break out of the prison of habit.

Making Friends with the Self

One of the happy consequences of growing older can be a gradual lessening of conflict and guilt. This is a welcome relief from the critical relationship to the self of adolescence (when idiosyncracies were grounds for mockery). By age forty, most of us have come to accept a great deal about ourselves; we aren't perfect, but we don't lose any sleep over it. Perhaps we like to watch trashy television programs, don't understand modern art, run out of energy at the end of the day, and enjoy a number of things we know are frivolous. We've had time to get used to these habits and feel that we've earned the right to indulge them. Yet when we uncover hidden parts of the self, we are often as critical of ourselves as a schoolyard full of teasing kids.

As a consequence, some of our self-awareness is anxious self-scrutiny, designed to eliminate or control what we imagine are flaws. We may realize that all our conversations are about ourselves, or that we have a constant need for reassurance, or that we can't seem to get along without a man (or a woman); we see ourselves bragging, whining, flirting, giving up easily, or maybe being afraid of honest confrontation. When we see ourselves revealed, we are tempted to draw back (just as we once did from our parents). We don't have to, though; we can make friends with the self.

Think of a friend. Most likely, you are aware of the friend's good qualities and bad. Knowing that you accept the whole package, the friend doesn't have to hide from you. Wouldn't it be nice to turn that attitude toward the self? to look upon personal foibles with the compassionate eyes of a friend? It can be done.

Cultivate an attitude of curiosity and interest about your fears and desires. Watch yourself alternately playing roles of strength and weakness. For example, you may discover that you thrive on people bringing their problems to you; or that you are reduced to childish defensiveness when someone gets angry; or that when you relax your usual self-reliant posture and ask someone for help, you begin to feel quite dependent on that person. Observe your moods swing back and forth from relaxed confidence to anxious self-doubt in various situations. Suspend your tendency to be self-critical; just notice. "When so-and-so does such-and-such I seem to react in a certain way. Hmmm, interesting."

"After my divorce I avoided going out," one person says, "because I always got so nervous on dates. Now I still get nervous, but I don't worry about it—and it passes." Another says, "In my thirties, I went through a whole series of friends. If the other person didn't call or I found out that she did things without inviting me, I felt so hurt and rejected that I stopped seeing her. At first when I switched from thinking 'you can't trust people' to 'I am insecure,' I felt terribly ashamed. But then I discovered that a lot of women feel the same way. I still feel bad if a friend rarely calls me. But now instead of dropping the friendship, I call."

Viewing ourselves in motion requires sympathetic detachment, which most of us can achieve better *after* the fact. You may, for example, realize that you overreacted to criticism only after you cool down. Cultivate the ability to pause between stimulus and response, but don't try to overcome every instinct, overreaction, and foolish impulse. Notice it later. Notice games, postures, and habits; see how they are manifest in your private thoughts and public behavior; notice the difference between yourself with men and with women.

Many of us restrict our natural spontaneity for fear of rejection. Often these fears persist unexamined because we are afraid to test them. A patient told me, "When I got to be forty I noticed that I started flirting more with women. You may not think there's anything wrong with that, but I remember how may father used to do it all the time, and how embarrassed I was. But then I realized I'm not my father. So instead of worrying about it, I give myself permission to be a little playful." There are two payoffs for hospitable self-awareness. The more we accept who we are, the more ready we are for full participation in life. Moreover, as we become aware of the nature of the roles we habitually perform, we are more likely to realize that alternative roles are available.

Taking full hold of life in the present leads us to relations with others. We have seen how low self-esteem inhibits easy and affectionate relations with others. It's hard to be neighborly when we are afraid. But we don't conquer one sphere and then the other. Making friends with the self and reaching out to others is an escalating spiral. The deeper we penetrate into our own secret hearts, the more open and unburdened we are in connection with others.

Breaking the Cycles of Habit

Many of our everyday interactions are constrained by recurring automatic behavior cycles. We notice how others impinge upon us, but it is hard, very hard, to see ourselves as acting and reacting members of systems. Maybe your husband turns on the television when you want to talk, or your boss takes your long hours for granted, or your wife has a tantrum every time you want to go off by yourself, or your lover expects you to drop everything when he calls. We want so desperately to change others that it is hard to let go of this linear view: *we* are unhappy because of what *they* do. The truth is that we are unhappy because of recurring cycles of what-we-do-and-they-do-and-we-do. We can change the system, but only by changing ourselves.

Think of the others as "starting it"; think of them as wrong; think of having to change yourself as unfair, if you like. All those who want "fair" can stop right here; those who want results read on.

Reflex reactions to feeling are what fix relationship patterns stubbornly in place. To behave more flexibly in a relationship system, you have to be able to operate counter to what feelings dictate. Most people hope that troublesome feelings will go away and make this a precondition for changing their behavior.

They think that in order not to withdraw, for example, they have to keep from feeling angry, or that they can't try something new if they are afraid to. In this way, we let feelings run our lives and ironically make feelings our enemy. Instead of fighting with your feelings ("I *shouldn't* get upset"), loosen the habit of automatically responding in certain ways. Pay attention to your habitual responses to anger, fear, pleasure, sexual feelings. Don't rush to analyze or change; noticing alone will enable you to start playing with options.

The interpersonal triangle is a useful concept, because it is a good way to differentiate process (how we relate) and content (what we talk about) in our thinking. Begin by observing triangular relationships in your own orbit. A relaxed, nonjudgmental attitude and not being in a hurry to change will help you to see more clearly. It may even be easier to see triangles that you aren't directly involved in. For example, you may notice how many of your colleagues clan together to bitch about the boss. Their doing so assumes that they can't make a direct impact on the boss; this in turn serves as a self-fulfilling prophesy. Not doing something preserves the fiction that you can't.

Some triangles are active products of our own creation. In response to rising anxiety we retreat and complain to others, avoiding personal confrontation and preventing resolution. Talking to a friend about a fight with your spouse may be consoling, but when it becomes a chronic pattern, the triangle freezes the relationship in place.

Sometimes we create triangles by intervening between others. Remembering the process of triangulation may help us to realize that the twosome can survive without our rescue efforts. If the kids are fighting, what so terrible could happen if we don't step in? If a husband starts arguing with his father on the way to the airport, do they really need a referee to smooth things over?

Give people back to each other to work out their own problems. "Sorry, kids, you'll have to settle it." "Talk to him; leave me out of it." "That's a shame; I'm sorry to hear that, but I think the two of you should talk it over." Most of us perpetuate at least one or two stalemated relationships by regularly complaining to someone else. Notice, for example, how many letters and phone calls contain displaced messages to third parties. We write to one friend about being slighted by another or call home to talk to one parent about the other.

Change is a three-step process: we change, other people signal us to "change back," and then we must maintain our changes. Often we change, but then are defeated by the other's reactions. If a woman stops nagging her teenage son to get up in the morning, he probably will be late for school—at least a couple of times. If a man starts spending Sunday afternoons with a family accustomed to getting along without him, they will likely resist his way of doing things. If you decide to start hugging your parents, it may make them uncomfortable for a while.

When we think of ourselves as part of a system, most of us confine our view to the small family circle. This is one reason for many people's tense preoccupation with *being* married or *being* single—as though our marital status controlled our fate. Countless people in midlife are convinced that they would be so much happier if only they were free of the entanglement of marriage or if only they could be married. This self-justification serves to excuse them from the burden of responsibility for their own destiny, and it restricts their vision to only one part of the large human family—the part, by the way, that may be least amenable to creative change in midlife. Trying to change is difficult as long as unresolved past relationships keep us stuck in place.

Parents: Going Back to the Source

Parents may represent the most important unfinished business of our lives. These relationships are the source of all subsequent relationships. Once we begin to resolve how we feel about our parents—the instant that begins to happen—we can start to relate to others. We may still have problems with other people, but when we are working on the relationship with a spouse or friend, we will be working on *that* relationship, instead of acting out or dramatizing the incomplete relationship with our parents. We're freeing ourselves from old business so we can get on to new business.

"But," one woman complained, "I *don't want to* work on my relationship with my mother; she criticized me terribly, and every time I see her the hurt continues. I can't handle it." This woman's entire life is dictated by her relationship to her mother. All of her relationships are shaped, molded, and limited by her unresolved fears of her mother. She runs toward anyone who praises her and hides from anyone who might criticize her. Until she completes her relationship with her mother, her life is very much about her relationship to her mother.

A thing is complete when you can allow it to be. If your mother treats you like a kid *and* you can't accept this, your life may be dominated by your attempt to make her stop treating you like a kid. Once you can let your mother be a person who treats you like a kid—in other words, accept the reality that she is who she is—then you don't have to fight it or organize your life around it.

When you are able to let your parents be exactly the way

they are, then you can complete your relationship with them —not when they become the way you want them to be or think they should be, because they are exactly the way they are. The same logic applies even if your parents are dead. Parents treating us like kids, or failing to spend time with us, or letting us down, or even dying: these are not the things that keep us stuck. Earlier I described the unsettling discovery that we can no longer depend on our parents. The truth is, we don't really *need* to depend on them anymore. We don't need them to take care of us, but we are still trying to change them. However, now that we have reached forty, an age many of us can remember them as being, it is easier to understand their lives and why they behave as they do. This lets us be the adults we are, instead of acting out the role of children we no longer are.

With apologies to Thomas Wolfe, we can and should go home again. A therapeutic odyssey back home teaches us how we developed many of the attitudes we have about ourselves and others, and it enables us to learn how to avoid overreacting when the family pushes our panic buttons. Incidentally, these two benefits go hand in hand. Becoming more objective about the forces that shaped us frees us from overreacting, and not overreacting makes us more objective. One visit home—if one remains calm enough to be objective—can teach more than six months of psychotherapy. If we watch and listen, we discover what we learned about having fun, being proud of ourselves, the expression of love, what women "should" do, what men "should" do, how close people "should" be, what topics of conversation are too frivolous or too personal, how one "should" express anger or good feelings, what makes us lovable, and what we "mustn't" do.

A woman friend of mine deliberately planned a visit home to discover the origins of some of her unshakable assumptions.

Observing the natives in her own habitat, she noticed that having fun is okay, but a woman should be ladylike (no loud laughter, no sweating or horsing around, and *certainly* no angry demands). Other messages were: selflessness and devotion meet with approval; conversations with men consist of getting them to talk about themselves. My friend knew these "beliefs" weren't rational, but it wasn't until she saw so clearly where they came from that she could begin to free herself from them.

Another friend discovered the following family myths during a short visit: being clever is more important than being sincere; it's not okay to brag; anger is dangerous; grown-ups don't get excited or show their feelings openly; serious is better than happy; asking for what you want is selfish; and fast is good, slow is bad. When we see our parents personifying these aspects of our self-image, we encounter the source of the narrators in our heads who engender so much self-doubt and worry. This makes it possible for us to shift from "My true self is unlovable" to "My mother has trouble showing love" or "My father gets uptight about some of the things I do."

After seeing how we are conditioned to hide or change who we are in response to what family members say, we can actually start reversing our defensive responses. We no longer have to choose between confrontation and apology. One woman said, "I come from a very strong-willed family. Being right means a lot. When my mother expressed an opinion, I felt that I had to either submerge my own ideas or fight with her. Even little things, like the correct time or what so-and-so said, were grounds for a struggle. Now when I go home I just say what I think; if someone doesn't agree, so what? I don't need to make them wrong for me to feel right."

Being yourself means owning your opinion and letting other people have theirs. It means being able to say "I don't know" and "I was wrong" without fear of invalidating yourself. The self grows enormously when we can respond on an adult level in situations that formerly rendered us so immature. Don't expect too much at the start; you're simply trying to break the mold. When your mother starts picking, stay calm and clear, and try reversing your usual reaction. Instead of some kneejerk defensive reaction, try letting your mother be right.

We handle important relationships in midlife in the same way we related to our families. Life may be playing grown-up, but most of us revert to childish roles when we get anxious. Those who were emotionally fused in their original families will repeat this pattern in the present. "I used to get upset when my husband wanted to do things without me," one woman said, "but seeing my parents' 'Siamese twin' act helped me to recognize where my reaction came from—*and* eventually to let go of it." Those who handled conflict by withdrawal or hysterical rages will continue to do so in the present. A colleague said: "When my boss chewed me out for not working up to potential, I was devastated. Then I got so mad I just wanted to quit. But after I cooled off, I could see myself acting like a kid. Instead of running away, I decided to show him what I can do."

People who distanced themselves from parents and siblings tend to rely on the same distancing mechanisms when tension mounts in their marriages. For example, a friend of mine told me, "When I'm upset with my husband, I withdraw and sulk. I dwell on my hurt feelings for a couple of days and punish him by ignoring him. I know it's immature and doesn't solve anything, but I keep doing it anyway." Another person said. "In emotional situations—happy or unhappy—I just start crying and can't express my feelings in words. It makes me feel so dumb!"

The following remarks may be more typical of men, but I have heard similar stories from women: "I come from a family where we didn't articulate our feelings. When I get mad at my wife I don't know what to say. Then it builds up inside me, and after a while something happens and I just start screaming at her. At those times I feel completely out of control, but I don't know how to stop it."

Getting divorced doesn't solve the problem; staying single doesn't prevent it. We retain our emotional vulnerabilities until we do something to resolve them—something like going back to their source.

Improving family relationships entails establishing personal, one-to-one relationships with as many members of the extended family as possible and changing one's role in the old scenario. This means reopening some relationships that have been dormant and learning to relate in new, healthier ways to "difficult" family members.

When you visit your family, take along kindness and forgiveness. Kindness lets you allow other people to be who they are, to think what they think and feel what they feel. Forgiveness enables you to let go of the resentment of what you think was and the fruitless longing for what could be.

Your mother talks a lot; your father doesn't understand you. The question is, are you willing to say, "That's the way things are," and let go of your preoccupation, your resentment, and your inability to accept that that's the way it is? "But she *really does . . . !*" and "He *never . . . !*" I know she really does, and he really never. The question is, are you willing to let go of your anger, self-righteousness, and self-pity? Are you willing to give up proving that you are right and they are wrong?

Learning to love is an exercise in accepting the truth that each of us is different and separate. We can even learn to enjoy the differences. Formerly "difficult" and "disagreeable" people begin to soften perceptibly as soon as we let them be who and what they are.

Try to realize that you are not changing the others, but *yourself* in relationship to them. The idea is not to make everybody happy or "tell the old man off." If your father is hypercritical, you aren't going to change him. But you can change the way you respond to that kind of treatment. Doing so will not only disarm your father's ability to drive you nuts, but also enable you to remain a calm, self-possessed adult when other people treat you as your father does.

Maybe you are thinking of a particular relationship now. Odds are that it is your relationship with one of your parents —the one that really bothers you. Perhaps it is an invasive mother who, no matter what you do, always seems to want more from you, or maybe a distancing father who draws back when you come near, shuts you out, and never answers when you offer your heart. Your relationship with this person, so important and so troublesome, may not be the best place to start. As long as you are trying something new, it makes sense to start off easy. Reestablishing contact with cutoff cousins or aunts and uncles may be easier and more immediately rewarding.

Closed relationships are often the best place to start because they are not so toxic with conflict and can help you to understand family patterns and reverse them. This proved to be the case for Gwen, whose father was a distancer, a man who could not tolerate much closeness.

"He rarely visits, seldom answers my letters, and usually seems annoyed or uncomfortable when I call. I keep trying, but he keeps pushing me away. . . . It hurts." After her divorce, when she needed to feel close to her family, Gwen spent a week in the country with an unmarried aunt, whom she hadn't seen in years. The aunt kept in touch with a huge network of kin and loved to tell family stories. Gwen was very attentive, especially when the narrative touched on her father. Gradually she learned how domineering her paternal grandmother had been, and that helped her to understand her father's need for a large bubble of emotional space. She also saw how much her father and her aunt were alike. The aunt denied her anger, but acted it out passively.

"One day we were shopping for some gloves and the saleslady waited on someone ahead of us," Gwen told me later. "When my aunt said, 'Can you help us,' the saleslady snapped, 'Just a minute, I'm busy.' My aunt grabbed me and said, 'Let's go,' and she has never been back to that store.

"My father is like that too. I remember how often he used to complain to us about this one or that one. But he didn't say anything directly to the people involved. I can see the same thing in myself. If someone starts smoking next to me in a restaurant I stare at them, thinking, 'If they had any sense they'd realize how annoying their smoking is.' Guess what? The only thing I accomplish is ruining my dinner."

It was a good week, as Gwen learned about the cycle of closeness and distance in her family. She could now see that her need for closeness pushed her father in his most vulnerable spot. Her calls and letters probably reminded him of his mother, always crowding him. As soon as Gwen understood that process, it lost some of its power to make her miserable. Gradually, she was able to develop a more rewarding relationship with her father by spending time with him but being more low-keyed. She was present but not pushy. As a result, he started inviting her to do things with him. He never did become truly expressive, but father and daughter became quite close.

Systems are tenacious, resistant to change; or to put it in more human terms, your parents have a long history of relating to you in a certain way. If you try to change that, you will be tense and their reaction will be intense. Have a plan when you visit them. When you feel yourself tightening up inside, your ability to observe and think about what is going on is markedly impaired. So it may be helpful to rehearse any new behavior you decide on beforehand; practice first in a relatively safe situation. Formulate reasonable goals. When you do test a new way of behaving, begin with behavior of moderate risk. Suppose, for example, you decide to start speaking up, instead of suffering inwardly, when your father starts putting people down. Don't wait until you blow up; don't make a big speech; just state your opinion calmly. Appraise the reaction of others to your changes; but remember, you take your position, let others take theirs.

The familiar adage "Two is company, three is a crowd" applies whenever you want to have a direct and honest relationship with someone. See your parents individually. Trying to talk to them together enables them to retreat into "we-ness" or pass the ball laterally. If you ask your father a difficult question, he can turn to your mother and say, "What do you think?"

It may not be easy to spend time alone with either of your parents. Here are some ways to do it: take your parent out to lunch; visit one when the other is away; take walks; or join in some other activity that one of them does alone. Sometimes it is necessary to come up with an excuse (!) for visiting with one of your parents. Interview them (separately) to help you write a personal family history; examine a family photograph album; or ask for advice, especially about something within one parent's purview. One of the best ways to establish a climate of emotional openness is to begin by opening yourself to the other person. Confidences beget confidences. By the way, it won't kill you to get advice, especially if (a) you solicit it and (b) you feel free to follow it or not.

Chances are one of your parents is a distancer, like Gwen's father. You may have to accept the distancing. On second thought, scratch the "may." Distancers are unsure of themselves and depend on privacy for self-protection. They try to prevent even those they love from getting too close. Pursuing distancers makes them anxious and frightens them away. This negative advice is important to keep in mind, but it doesn't solve the problem. You will have to be creative in working out the details. In general, move slowly, and don't push. For example, plan brief visits; give distancers plenty of time to anticipate your visit (for this reason, letters are better than phone calls). Surprise company causes automatic anxiety in distancers.

It may help to realize that there are levels of intimacy: from contact, to chitchat, to semipersonal topics, to personal conversations about things that are important to each of you, to intimate discussions of matters that are usually private, to talking about the relationship. Move slowly from one level to the next, and stop when either of you becomes too anxious. Don't push the conversation to a level where the other person is uncomfortable.

Patrick longed for a more personal relationship with his mother, but she seemed allergic to intimacy. Occasionally he would pour out his heart to her in a letter, telling her about his life, asking about hers, and saying how much he wished they could be closer. She seldom answered. Then he felt hurt and angry, and for a long time only made superficial contact with her. When he visited, he talked mostly to his father. In other words, Patrick alternated between two extremes of intimacy.

Once he understood this pattern he was able to make significant progress. He invited his mother out to lunch and limited his conversation to neutral subjects—the weather, the restaurant, and the President's latest gaffes. Because she was not pushed beyond her comfort zone, Patrick's mother was able to relax and enjoy herself. In fact, she took a small step herself, by asking Patrick about his work and then telling him some details about hers. On subsequent occasions, Patrick moved toward more personal subjects, including some problems with his children. He was also able to ask his mother about the early years of her marriage. By noticing when his mother began to be uncomfortable, he was able to moniter her level of anxiety and back off from certain subjects. But they were making progress.

Parents who pursue are even harder to cope with. They put us on the defensive; it's hard to stop running away when we feel someone trying to smother us. The first thing to realize is that it isn't just "them" pursuing "us"; it is an interlocking pattern of pursuit and withdrawal. What would happen if we stopped running away, stayed put, and said, "Take me, I'm yours"? It may feel as though the pursuing parents would eat us alive, but they won't.

David's widowed mother visited only about twice a year, but he dreaded it. If he had a meeting after work, she complained that he was avoiding her. If he took a day off from work to spend with her, she wanted two. And she always had plenty of advice about the kids. "You shouldn't push them so hard. So what if they don't do their homework, they want to be with Grandma." For years he avoided her and she complained.

Then, as he told me, "I tried something completely different. *I* visited her. It was my wife's idea; I didn't think it would work, but agreed to try anyway. I chose a three-day weekend and decided to spend as much time with her as she wanted. She was thrilled! She showed me off to all her friends, she took me shopping, and together we visited my father's grave." Much to his surprise, David found that when he made himself more available to his mother, she didn't really want all of his time. "I have things to do myself, you know," she reminded him.

The world is not made up of two distinct species, pursuers and distancers. We all tend to pursue in some areas, distance in others, and to pursue more of the time in some relationships, while distancing in others. Pursuing and distancing are patterns, not traits. Instead of always being on the defensive with a pursuing parent—waiting until he or she comes near and then withdrawing—pick your own time and place and subject, and initiate the contact. This breaks the pattern in a way that leaves you more comfortable and in control.

For example, if your mother annoys you with frequent phone calls or visits during which she pumps you for information about your latest boyfriend or your job (or whatever subject you don't want to be bugged about), try calling or visiting her, and bring up something you would be more comfortable talking about. Ask her about herself. Discuss family history, and ask her about her feelings. Remember, though, to avoid the temptation to change her; what works is accepting her, changing yourself in relationship to her.

Don't expect to understand interchanges while they are taking place. There is one principal figure in the situation you can't see. At least one. Probably two. Later you'll have time to reflect. Personal change of any kind proceeds in steady small steps. We need to plunge forward and then reflect on our experience. All reflecting and no experience makes us neurotic; all experience and no reflection makes us servants of habit and impulse.

Revitalizing Love Relationships

Understanding your parents may not magically transform your relationships with them, but it brings a sense of completion and a release. It is also possible to make breakthroughs with spouses, lovers, or friends, but these relationships may require more continuous attention.

By the time we arrive at midlife many of us are chronically disappointed in our intimate relationships, especially those with lovers or spouses. This can be true whether or not we have a long-standing "primary relationship"—whether we are married or single. The less fully developed our sense of self, the more threatening is intimacy. Many of us learn to negotiate around this threat by steering clear of difficult relationships or settling into complacent habits.

The routines that make for a comfortable and predictable haven may erode the spontaneity of a marriage. After a while, people take each other for granted. Communication gradually fades away or sinks into a rut. What do people in stagnant relationships do to keep them stuck? They avoid conflict; they have fixed images of their partners and of the relationship; and they don't consider themselves as part of the equation. Then they turn away from what they consider a hopeless situation and invest their energy elsewhere.

Husbands and wives still talk, of course, but usually about a narrow range of subjects, often practical ("Can we afford a vacation?"), or they talk about the children, if there are any ("What time did you tell him to be home?"). When they do talk about things that are important to them, settled couples usually only go so far and then they break off the discussion. This works like the cybernetic set point on the heating system —the idea is to avoid, at all costs, the possibility of getting overheated.

When was the last time you sat down with your spouse and told him or her exactly what you were feeling? There may be several reasons why it has been a long time. "There isn't enough time"; "he's always watching television"; "she isn't interested." Opening up communication is partly a matter of just doing it, of taking the risk to be more straightforward, alive, and real with each other. But let me also make two suggestions. First, you need to get your partner's attention. The best way *not* to be heard is to attempt to have a serious conversation in the midst of everyday routine or to interrupt your partner's reading, watching television, or paying the bills. The best chance for conversation occurs when the two of you are away from competing distractions. Going for a walk or out to dinner is conducive to talking more openly.

Another thing to remember is that your relationship is governed by a mutual exchange. Most of us are so preoccupied with what *we* want in our relationships, what's missing for us, that we overlook what the other person wants from us. Some couples don't talk much, because neither one listens. Probably the best way to reopen communication is to give your partner the chance to talk freely and without interruption.

Some people have trouble listening; they assume they have to *do something* if their partners have a problem. If your mate complains about the job, show your concern by listening sympathetically, *not* by giving advice. If you say, "Why don't you quit?" or "It couldn't be that bad" your partner will learn that it isn't safe to open up. If you have a problem, you can help others to listen by letting them know that's all you need: "I know you can't do anything about it, but I want to tell you about a problem I'm having at work"; or "I'm upset and I wish you would just listen."

Reciprocity is the key to satisfaction in relationships. Show the other person that you care and are concerned about his or her well-being. Compassionate sensitivity is an expansion of the self, an ability to feel what others feel, consider what they need, and put oneself out, when necessary, to respond to their needs and feelings. Psychologists call it "giving to get," and it works.

Our own yearning for love may be so strong that we think primarily of our own feelings. But what is the other person feeling, that cruel monster who selfishly withholds the little sympathy we crave? Perhaps that person also feels neglected and is hurt and angry—not necessarily about what we are doing; maybe about any of a hundred other things.

A woman patient said to me, "The other day I was feeling neglected by my husband. We had a bad week, snapping at each other, and now he was ignoring me. Just then my twelve-year-old daughter came in and said, 'Mommy, I wish somebody would write me a letter. I haven't heard from Grandma in weeks.' So I told her what parents have been telling their kids for generations: 'Why don't *you* write to her, sweetheart; people who write letters get letters.' Then it dawned on me, maybe I could apply some of that advice myself. The next day I bought a card and wrote in it 'I know you're under a lot of pressure. I'm sorry. I miss you' and left it in my husband's mailbox at lunchtime. He called me later in the afternoon, so pleased. The cycle was broken. That night we went out to dinner and had one of the best times we've had in a long time."

In order for a relationship system to continue unchanged, all members must play their part. However, most of us think that relationships will not improve because the others will never change. Once we are willing to give up the sweet solace of seeing ourselves as innocent victims, we can discover the roles we play in maintaining the status quo.

If you aren't getting what you want, think of yourself as a stimulus. You may still *feel* like a victim, but consider what you might be doing to bring about the reaction you get from those around you. If your spouse avoids conversations with you, consider what you may be doing that he or she doesn't like.

Do you nag? Nagging is a form of *aversive control*—punishing the other person to get what you want. Other examples of aversive control are crying, withdrawing, threatening, cross-complaining, and name-calling. These angry responses usually only escalate the problem. Either your mate responds in kind or stays away altogether. Instead of nagging ("reminding," "giving helpful suggestions") or suffering in silence, say what you feel. But limit your complaints to those things that directly affect you, those you really care about. Avoid bringing up the past and what you wish the other person *wouldn't* do. Make simple, declarative statements about what you do want.

One woman wished she could spend more time alone with her husband. But that's all she did, wish. She assumed he wasn't interested—and wasn't sure she "deserved" the time away from the children. (We want our spouses to know what we want, and to follow through voluntarily and spontaneously.) Finally she said to him: "Honey, I'd like to take a few weekend trips this summer. Just the two of us." His response was, "Sure, that sounds like a great idea."

As easy as that? Yes, sometimes. Assuming that you can't get what you want and so not bothering to ask is more than "passivity" or "laziness" (these are labels, not explanations). It is *projective identification*—that is, you project your own conflicts —in the instance above, about having fun—onto the nearest target.

Are you always talking about your work and never asking about your partner's work? Do you criticize too much? You don't know? Ask. The point is not to substitute self-blame for blame projected outward, but to get away from blaming altogether. Instead of thinking that X (your family's rejection) causes Y (your hurt feelings), think of a reciprocal relationship where your behavior and their behavior are linked in an ongoing circular pattern: X-Y-X-Y-X, and so on. It doesn't matter how things got started; what matters is what you do about them.

Most of the couples I see in therapy go through a predictable sequence. First, they blame each other. "He never wants to have anybody over." "She won't let me have any time for myself." Then (with a little encouragement) they start communicating what they feel and making requests. "I miss spending time with my friends. I wish you would help me plan an occasional dinner party." "I need some time by myself. Why don't you and the kids do something without me once in a while on the weekend?" But then, having expressed themselves, they often wait for the other one to change. You can keep from getting stuck by making the first move. If you give your spouse more of what he or she wants, it will come back to you.

One busy couple, who wanted to infuse their relationship with more intimacy, decided to make special time to be together. So, once a week they read good fiction aloud to each other before a roaring fire. Another couple started going to the movies and discussing them afterward over wine and cheese. A third set a scheduled time for a "date" once a month (without the children) and made sure they had no other commitments at this time.

Some people balk at the idea of structured exercises in intimacy. "We shouldn't need structure," they believe. Fine. We should be spontaneous, open, honest, and free. But real change is made only within the confines of our own limitations. We may need the props, and many people find that some form of structure helps sustain change.

Reaching Out for Friendship

Expanding our circle of friends has the same double benefit as improving family relationships: we strengthen the self and enlarge our active relationship system. But most likely the relative value changes. Friendship is a warm, receptive, somewhat less complicated relationship in which to nurture the hidden parts of the self. With friends, we learn to be ourselves.

Friends help us in many ways, sometimes doing things for us, sometimes doing things with us. A companion helps ease the strain of an exercise class and sustains the commitment to keep going. I know a group of middle-aged men, who playfully call themselves "The Willow Street Gang," who run together every Sunday morning. For most of them the twelve-mile Sunday run is the longest effort of the week, and there are two very steep hills to make it tougher. The group has evolved an informal tradition that whenever they come to one of these hills, someone in the group tells a joke. This homey example helps illustrate how friends help each other share the load.

"Networking" is a recent alternative for the kind of support people used to find in family and friends. Like-minded people come together now in women's groups, men's groups, cooperative playgroups, Parents without Partners, and so on. You may be surprised to discover how many of these groups already exist in your neighborhood and how easy it is to start new ones. The willingness of so many people to participate demonstrates a growing recognition that we need each other *and* that we may have to make special efforts to find the kind of fellowship that once came more naturally.

A male friend wrote me recently, "Five years ago I would have turned up my nose at the idea of joining a men's group. I wasn't ready to think about things like friendship and learning to relax, and I definitely wasn't ready to acknowledge my need for a structured format to improve the quality of my life. Now I'm glad I joined the group. We talk about a lot of things —work, sex, kids—I suppose it's a little like therapy. Sometimes it's an effort to go. I am by nature somewhat shy, and when things get me down my inclination is to be by myself. But my commitment to the group has helped me overcome my tendency to withdraw into my shell. Attending the group is one of the most rewarding things I've ever done for myself."

Mature friendships must be given a special priority. Many of us have to learn to stop letting work or other obligations automatically take precedence over the people we care about. If friends come second, we risk losing the pleasure of their company, and sometimes their trust, as the following vignette illustrates.

When Doug agreed to meet his old friend Sharon at five o'clock, he penciled the time in his appointment book. Later, when a client requested a meeting "sometime in the next couple of days," Doug gave away the five o'clock time, temporarily forgetting the drink with Sharon. When Sharon called to confirm, he apologized, explaining that "something had come up at work." She said, "That's okay, how about sometime next week?"

Friends forgive, but they aren't immune from hurt. If Doug makes a habit of putting friends off, he won't have them when he decides he wants them.

Enhancing friendships means not only making time, but also becoming more open. Human identity consists of two elements: a sense of belonging and a sense of being separate.

Ironically, those who yearn most for belonging often cut themselves off from others to protect fragile self-esteem. Their exaggerated autonomy, which begins as a defense, may actually provide the illusion of independent strength. Eventually—and especially in midlife—they begin to realize their dependent longings. "Thank God I discovered this while there was still time to do something about it," one patient admitted to me.

Friendships can get stuck when friends have hurt feelings and wait for the other person to make the first move. The sad thing is that the friendship can dry up while each is waiting for the other to reach out. When this happens it may take a gutsy confrontation to clear the air. Afraid to say what might offend or disappoint, we weigh the choices—"Should I tell her, or will she get mad?"—and often don't dare. But disaster seldom strikes if we honestly communicate thoughts and reservations. As follows:

Linda hadn't heard from Martha for some time. Normally, the two friends saw each other two or three times a week, but since Martha's marriage she seldom called. Linda began to wonder if Martha was letting their friendship go. She had invited Martha and Ned over for dinner twice, but they hadn't reciprocated.

The problem here is that Martha, having married, has become a couple and the Noah's Ark syndrome (animals two by two) is at work. She and Ned have thought about having Linda over several times, but it didn't seem to work out. Once they were going to invite her to a party, but since Linda didn't have a man to bring they thought they had to find someone for her. (Unfortunately, social conventions are slow to change.) Another time they tried to arrange dinner with an extra person to even things out, but most of the people they knew were paired off.

Although Linda was worried about Martha's reaction, she

invited Martha out to lunch and told her just how she felt. She was hurt, she said, but reluctant to say so for fear of alienating Martha. (This second part of the message makes it very clear that no attack is intended.) As it turned out, Martha was relieved, not defensive. She too was worried about the friendship. She missed their talks, shopping trips, and visits to the art gallery. It *was* hard to find time for her friends now that she was married, but the fact that Linda cared enough to confide her hurt helped Martha realize that this was one friend worth making time for.

Pseudo-Friendships

True friendship is mutual, yet many of us get trapped into squandering our valuable time with those who happen to seek us out or "need us." A surprising number of us put petitioners for advice and solicitors for worthy causes ahead of our friends. (This is the superego at work.) Real friends, of course, also turn to each other for advice and comfort, but in a friendship of equals one person does not always lean on the other.

Some people even use suffering as the basis for friendships. As one woman told me, "I always prided myself on being sympathetic; my relationships revolved around helping other people with what's bothering them—usually relationships with someone else. I made time for anyone with a problem, feeling a little obligated (and a little self-righteous). Recently, however, I decided I was cheating myself out of genuine friendship. Taking the maternal role was safe; I didn't have to expose myself—*my* fears, *my* needs, *my* feelings. Oh, I'm still willing to lend a sympathetic ear, but lately I'm likely to be busy with friends."

In order to make room in our lives for rewarding friendships, we may have to extricate ourselves from relationships that are destructive, draining, or have simply run their course. Relationships based primarily on habit or obligation aren't friendships. Instead of using pseudo-friendships to give us a sense of being sought after, it may make more sense to limit friendships to those that are genuine. Decide which friendships provide enjoyment, acceptance, trust, respect, and mutual assistance. These are the real friendships.

Make time for your friends; ask favors and grant them. Write letters. Visit when you can. Let your friends know who and what you are. That seems to be the hard part—preserving a sense of self and at the same time closing the distance. It involves saying, "I am me. Anything you offer as a directive, I will accept as nonbinding advice." That way you can hear your friends, without fear of being taken over. You don't have to fight against pressure if you aren't afraid you might succumb to it. This is easier with friends than with family.

Being a friend means being able to say no. You don't have to take over your friend's responsibility. If you know that and your friends know that, it is easier for friends to ask for what they want and for you to hear it without feeling threatened by demands.

Friendship may lack the ardent passion of romance, but for that reason it is gentler and more constant. We may fret about our families and our lovers, but with our friends we are easy. In friendship we feel uncomplicated love. It is a unique situation.

Recently I read that the Chinese ideogram for crisis is the same as the one for opportunity. I liked the idea because it suggests that the thesis of this book is rooted in the wisdom of an ancient people. But when I tried to authenticate what I read, I could not. Two Chinese professors told me that it simply wasn't true, the words are different. Then I learned that in Mandarin Chinese the images for crisis and opportunity are structurally similar. Crisis does not equal opportunity, but you can turn crisis into opportunity.

That fits well with my experience. Wisdom means accepting what is; it does not, however, mean passive acquiescence. We can take a time of crisis in stride and turn it into creative living by accepting the inevitable strains and dealing with life as it comes, rather than bemoaning that it isn't the way it should be.

Life itself is not a problem to be solved. Life is something to be lived, as wisely and as well as we can, day in and day out. Life is something to savor and enjoy. There is no solution for it, but to live it. We live it today; and tomorrow morning, when we wake up, we live it again.

Bibliography

Bernard, Jessie. *The Future of Marriage*. New York: Bantam, 1973.

Blumstein, Philip, and Schwartz, Pepper. *American Couples*. New York: Morrow, 1983.

Bodin, Jeanne, and Mitelman, Bonnie. *Mothers Who Work: Strategies for Coping*. New York: Ballantine Books, 1983.

Bowen, Murray. *Family Therapy in Clinical Practice*. New York: Jason Aronson, 1978.

Cutler, William, Garcia, C., and Edwards, D. *Menopause: A Guide for Women and the Men Who Love Them*. New York: Norton, 1983.

Ehrenreich, Barbara. *The Hearts of Men*. Garden City, NY: Anchor Press, 1983.

Erikson, Erik. *Childhood and Society*. New York: Norton, 1950.

————. *Identity, Youth and Crisis*. New York: Norton, 1968.

Freud, Sigmund. The Interpretation of Dreams (1900). Vols. 4 and 5 in *The Standard Edition of the Complete Psychological Works of*

Sigmund Freud, trans. and ed. by James Strachey. New York: Norton, 1976.

————. "Instincts and Their Vicissitudes" (1915). Vol. 14, pp. 111–40 in *The Standard Edition.*

————. "The Ego and the Id" (1923). Vol. 19, pp. 1–60 in *The Standard Edition.*

————. "Inhibitions, Symptoms and Anxiety" (1926). Vol. 20, pp. 75–173 in *The Standard Edition.*

Fried, Barbara. *The Middle-Age Crisis.* New York: Harper & Row, 1967.

Friedan, Betty. "Feminism Takes a New Turn." *The New York Times Magazine,* November 18, 1979.

Gilligan, Carol. *In a Different Voice.* Cambridge, MA: Harvard University Press, 1982.

Ginott, Haim. *Between Parent and Child.* New York: Avon, 1969.

Gould, Roger. *Transformations: Growth and Change in Adult Life.* New York: Simon and Schuster, 1978.

Guerin, Philip. *Family Therapy: Theory and Practice.* New York: Gardner Press, 1976.

Hetherington, Mavis, Cox, M., and Cox, R. "Divorced Fathers." *Family Coordinator* 25, (1976): 417–28.

Jackson, Don. "Family Rules: Marital Quid Pro Quo." *Archives of General Psychiatry* 12, (1965): 589–94.

Jaques, Elliot. "Death and the Mid-Life Crisis." *International Journal of Psychoanalysis* 46 (1965): 502–14.

Jung, Carl. *Modern Man in Search of a Soul.* New York: Harcourt Brace, 1933.

Kinsey, Alfred, Pomeroy, W., and Martin, C. *Sexual Behavior in the Human Male.* Philadelphia: W. B. Saunders, 1948.

Kohut, Heinz. *The Analysis of the Self*. New York: International Universities Press, 1971.

———. *The Restoration of the Self*. New York: International Universities Press, 1977.

Levinson, Daniel. *The Seasons of a Man's Life*. New York: Ballantine Books, 1978.

Lidz, Theodore. *The Person: His and Her Development Throughout the Life Cycle*. New York: Basic Books, 1976.

Mahler, Margaret, Pine, F., and Bergman, A. *The Psychological Birth of the Human Infant*. New York: Basic Books, 1975.

Masson, Jeffrey. *The Assault on Truth: Freud's Suppression of the Seduction Theory*. New York: Farrar, Straus & Giroux, 1984.

Miller, Jean Baker. *Toward a New Psychology of Women*. Boston: Beacon Press, 1976.

Miller, Stuart. *Men and Friendship*. Boston: Houghton Mifflin, 1983.

Minuchin, Salvador. *Families and Family Therapy*. Cambridge, MA: Harvard University Press, 1974.

Nichols, Michael. *Family Therapy: Concepts and Methods*. New York: Gardner Press, 1983.

Scarf, Maggie. *Unfinished Business: Pressure Points in Women's Lives*. New York: Doubleday, 1980.

Schofield, William. *Psychotherapy: The Purchase of Friendship*. Englewood Cliffs, NJ: Prentice-Hall, 1964.

Sheehy, Gail. *Passages: Predictable Crises of Adult Life*. New York: E. P. Dutton, 1976.

———. *Pathfinders*. New York: Bantam, 1982.

Terkel, Studs. *Working*. New York: Pantheon, 1972.

Thompson, Clara. " 'Penis Envy' in Women." In *Interpersonal Psy-*

choanalysis: The Selected Papers of Clara M. Thompson, edited by Maurice Green. New York: Basic Books, 1964.

Turkle, Sherry. *The Second Self.* New York: Simon and Schuster, 1984.

Vaillant, George. *Adaptation to Life.* Boston: Little, Brown, 1977.

Index